In the
Best Interests of
the Child

The professional participants in the child placement process do not, either separately or together, make or make up for a parent.

In the Best Interests of the Child

Professional Boundaries

JOSEPH GOLDSTEIN
Law School, Yale University

ANNA FREUD
Director
Hampstead Child-Therapy Clinic,

ALBERT J. SOLNIT
Child Study Center, Yale University

SONJA GOLDSTEIN
Arthur Sachs, Schpero, Berman
& Shure, New Haven

THE FREE PRESS
A Division of Macmillan, Inc.
New York

COLLIER MACMILLAN PUBLISHERS
London

The Free Press
A Division of Macmillan, Inc.
866 Third Avenue, New York, N. Y. 10022

Collier Macmillan Canada, Inc.

Printed in the United States of America

printing number

1 2 3 4 5 6 7 8 9 10

Library of Congress Cataloging-in-Publication Data
Main entry under title:

In the best interests of the child.

 Bibliography: p.
 Includes index.
 1. Custody of children—United States. 2. Parent and
child (Law)—United States. 3. Child welfare—United
States. I. Goldstein, Joseph.
KF547.I5 1986   346.7301'7   85-16250
ISBN 0-02-912180-9   347.30617
ISBN 0-02-912380-1 (pbk.)

To
Dorothy Burlingham

Contents

x   Contents

Preface

This book, one in a series by these authors addressed to the best interests of children in custody and placement situations, should make those of us now involved in such work look closely at ourselves and the way in which we approach and carry out our professional roles. For those entering the field it is an introduction to the challenges, complexities, and dangers that lie along the paths traversed by clinical and legal decision makers. The authors have taken a giant step toward the delineation of practices for improving the lives of children who come to our attention.

The very beginning of the book sets the tone, opening with the statement that "The professional participants in the child placement process do not, either separately or together, make or make up for a parent." The final chapter is an eloquent summation of the attitudes, behavior, and wisdom the authors counsel us to strive for in the best interests of our child clients and patients: to recognize the crucial importance of the "ordinary devoted parent," to distinguish between professionally informed belief and personal value preferences; to refrain from exceeding one's competence and authority; to learn to work with others who have responsibilities in the child placement process; to avoid the dangers of assuming dual roles in a single case; to recognize the difference between the caring expert and the usurper of parental authority; to be unafraid to incorporate the view that good professional practice requires softheartedness as well as hardheadedness.

The authors have brought to this book their sophistication as theoreticians of law and psychoanalysis and as practitioners with years of hands-on experience dealing with child placement issues and problems. An integral part of the process through which they have arrived at the present writing has been the Child Placement Conflicts Seminar at the Yale Child Study Center. As a participant with Joseph and Sonja Goldstein and Albert Solnit in those meetings since 1977, I am vividly aware of the process through which our group of lawyers, child psychiatrists, pediatricians, psychologists, and social workers struggled as each of us tried to clarify our professional responsibilities and boundaries around the real life cases with which we were concerned. The discussions were wide-ranging in scope, certainly heated, and sometimes combative as we presented and argued about the clinical material, the social situations, the possible options, and the tasks we had undertaken. The complexity and poignancy of many of the situations—some horrendous beyond imagining—the fact that in many situations there was no solution that seemed beneficial for all parties involved, our dissatisfaction at the imperfections of our

knowledge and our systems of care and protection
beset us and often outweighed any satisfaction we
might feel at having contributed to a constructive or
least detrimental plan for a child. The clarity and conviction with which the issues are defined in this book,
I believe, owe much to the fact that they were fired in
the crucible of these seminars.

In the early years of their existence the seminar
sessions were intense and exhausting. The reasons for
the intensity and exhaustion, beyond the usual concerns about whether one has performed competently
as a professional under the scrutiny of one's colleagues, can be clearly understood when one reflects
upon the issues dealt with in this book. But an interesting and relieving state gradually came into being in the seminars at least among the veteran members. Though the individual cases are now no less
complex and difficult or just plain awful, we have arrived at a stage in our professional growth when we
experience the situations and feelings they engender
as signals that alert us to problems without overwhelming us and that suggest certain professional
directions and procedures based on what we have
learned about child placement.

Among many important points made in this
book there are two that in my view are of special
significance for even the most experienced and competent professionals: the warning against the danger
of allowing personal values to distort professional
decisions, and the hazards of trying to perform dual
roles in reference to one case. It may well be that we
have the greatest difficulty in learning to resist the

temptation to allow personal preferences to modify or determine professional judgment. It is a task more difficult than achieving reasonable mastery of the knowledge base of our professional practice. The risk of deciding what one prefers, then looking for data that support the preference can be so insidious as to capture the unwary. It is not easy for any of us to keep such things straight, especially since professional knowledge and personal values at times coincide. Because the hope that parents and children will not be lost to each other is very strong in most of us, there are times when hopes and wishes weaken carefully considered scientifically based opinions. One way of guarding against the clinical errors of wishful thinking is to share responsibilities with colleagues having agreed on the task each will undertake and helping each other to keep the roles clearly defined.

This book is, in the best sense, a state-of-the-art discussion and shows how many of our practices can immediately be improved while looking toward a continuing refinement in our professional knowledge.

SALLY PROVENCE

Anna Freud's Part in This Book

Anna Freud participated in the writing of this book from its beginning in 1979 until shortly before her death in October 1982.

Acknowledgments

Many individuals and several institutions have encouraged and facilitated our writing of this book. We wish to acknowledge our appreciation for their support.

For critical comment and elbow-to-elbow editorial help on various drafts of the manuscript: Jane W. Ellis, Catherine Mary Newell, and Paul Michael Schwartz.

For their thoughts and suggestions: Judith Areen, Daniel Braverman, Fredericka Breneman, E. Donald Elliott, Henry A. Finlay, Owen M. Fiss, Joshua Goldstein, Kathryn Lowell, Sophie Lowenstein, Martha L. Minow, Donn Pickett, Sally Provence, James and Joyce Robertson, Nancy Schwartz, Spiros Simitis, Ben Solnit, Dean and Marie Tegeler, Philip Tegeler, and Stephen Wizner; and the participants in the Child Placement Conflicts Seminar, Yale Child Study Center, 1977–1984, and in the Family Law Seminar, Yale Law School, Fall 1982.

For encouragement and a setting in which to think and work: Harry Wellington, Dean, Yale Law School; Robert Berliner and Leon Rosenberg, Deans, Yale School of Medicine; Aubrey L. Diamond, Director, Institute of Advanced Legal Studies, London University; Anne Bohm, Secretary of the Graduate School, The London School of Economics; and Arthur S. Sachs, senior partner of the law firm Arthur Sachs, Schpero, Berman & Shure.

For careful and thoughtful editing: Lottie M. Newman.

For indexing: Bonny Hart.

For patient, good-humored, creative, and precise processing of manuscript to book: George A. Rowland.

For library assistance: Robert E. Brooks, Donald Carter, Martha Clark, Morris L. Cohen, Gene Coakley, Tony Henderson, Mike Hughes, James Kennealy, and Sandra Trent.

For unstinting, cheerful, imaginative, and highly skilled preparation of the many drafts of manuscript: Juliana Flower, Dolores T. Gee, Elizabeth H. Sharp, and Elizabeth Voionmaa.

For secretarial and photocopying assistance: Gina Bon, Russ Hentz, Joanne E. Kittredge, and Walter Moriarty.

For generous and gratifying sustenance at all of our London meetings: Paula Fichtl.

For travel, study, and research grants: Elizabeth Dollard, The Free Press, Edna McConnell Clark Foundation, Saul Z. and Amy S. Cohen Family Foundation, John Simon Guggenheim Memorial Foundation, Irving B. Harris Foundation, and Florence and John Schuman Foundation.

Concerning the Material in This Book

Much of the material in this book is drawn from the clinical experience of the authors and their participation in the review of case reports prepared by colleagues. With the exception of matters in the public domain, the names, other identifying characteristics of individuals, and the time and place of events have been changed, and statements and conversations have been combined and reconstructed.

Part One

The Professional
and Child Placement

Chapter 1

The Problem and Our Questions

Parents raise their children as a labor of love and not as a professional assignment. Unlike child development experts and other professional persons concerned with child care, parents are not specialists. Their responsibility is the whole child—his every need at all times. Ordinary devoted parents[1] "accept his love, tolerate his demands and failings, share his pain and pleasure—and get satisfaction from doing so. They may be sorely tried at times, but more than anyone else they are able to tolerate his growing pains. The child knows he is special to them, whether he is pleasing or not, well or ill, succeeding or failing. He unhesitatingly turns to them with his pleasure and miseries, confident that they will be there. He knows they are likely to see his point of view and give him the benefit of doubt before voicing critical comment. They become the brick wall he can safely kick against. Impatient or angry though they may some-

3

times be, he recognizes that these are often signs of their concern for him. His feelings about himself reflect his parents' feeling about him. The child whose parents value him values himself. Parents usually carry these strong feelings throughout their lives—the love, the anxiety for their children's welfare and happiness."*

Acknowledging the unique place of such ordinary devoted parents, the law safeguards their rights to raise their children as they think best. That is why parental autonomy and family privacy are respected and why, for example, parents are usually relied upon to decide what is in the best interests of their child, including whether and when to seek professional assistance. The law also recognizes that there are situations when, on behalf of the child, the state is justified in breaching family privacy and supervening parental autonomy.[3] Then the child placement process is invoked and the all-encompassing parental task is broken up and temporarily divided among specialists from law, medicine, child development, child care, social work, education, and other professions concerned with children and their families.† It is in the best interests of the child that these professionals always keep in mind that they are not the child's parents. Even though each of them

---

*The words are those of the English child development experts, James and Joyce Robertson.[2]

†"Child placement, for our purposes, is a term which encompasses all legislative, judicial and executive decisions generally or specifically concerned with establishing, administering or rearranging parent–child relationships."[4]

may assume one or more aspects of the parental task, neither alone nor together can they replace parents.

Professional persons know that the ultimate goal of the placement process is to provide children with parents who will be free from further state intrusion—free to use or refuse their help, free to accept or reject their interventions. Yet the tragic situations that they often confront in child placement cases tend to blur their awareness of their own limitations and the limits of their assignments. Their personal experiences and sympathies sometimes interfere with their professional judgment. And their effort to maintain a purely professional stance carries with it the risk that they may become wooden and lose the humanity that is essential to good work with children and their families.

We did not examine this professional quandary in either *Beyond the Best Interests of the Child* or *Before the Best Interests of the Child.* There we introduced and developed the least detrimental alternative standard for child placement.* We defined the functions of state intervention and the justifications for authorizing the state to modify parent–child relationships. Here we develop further that component of the least detrimental alternative which mandates

---

*"The least detrimental alternative . . . is that specific placement and procedure for placement which maximizes, in accord with the child's sense of time and on the basis of short-term predictions given the limitations of knowledge, his or her opportunity for being wanted and for maintaining on a continuous basis a relationship with at least one adult who is or will become his (or her) psychological parent."[5]

that placement decisions take into account the limits of knowledge about child development and the law's inability to supervise day-to-day parent–child relationships. We examine, from the vantage point of the children caught up in the placement process, the work of those professionals—legislators, lawyers, judges, social workers, child development experts, and child care agency administrators—who determine whether parents have failed or who plan, provide, order or supervise alternative care for children. We seek to clarify their relationship to each other and to the families they serve, to identify good practices as well as situations where even the best of them are tempted to step outside of their professional roles and exceed their authority or fail to discharge their obligations.

In *Beyond the Best Interests of the Child,* we warned against attributing to judges, to lawyers, to social workers, to child psychiatrists, and to other professionals in the process "a magical power—a power to do what is far beyond their means."[6] In *Before the Best Interests of the Child,* we stressed the importance of considering "what a child loses when he passes, even temporarily, from the personal authority of parents to the impersonal authority of the law."[7] Here we take as a given that the professional participants in the process accept these limits and share these concerns. We believe that they would agree that they *ought not* to exceed their authority and *ought not* to go beyond or counter to their special knowledge or training. But we do not take for granted that they always recognize when they go or are asked to go beyond their limits. Sometimes they do not recognize that they are doing what they "know" they ought not to do. This may be because the law gives them vague and ambiguous assignments; because they have a strong desire to help people in trouble; because they feel a need to justify their work; because they desire to avoid the embarrassment of acknowledging that they do not know; because they do not pause to consider whether they are being asked to exceed their professional qualifications; or because of a combination of these and other less obvious or, perhaps, less understandable reasons. Though we do sometimes speculate about the *why* of professional behavior, we do not systematically explore such explanations. Our primary goal is to identify and describe situations *when* judges, lawyers, child psychiatrists, social workers, and other nonparent participants in the child placement process stay or fail to stay within the limits of their knowledge, training, or authority.

To do this we address several questions which we explore separately and which merit consideration by the professionals themselves, by those who engage their services, and by the families they serve:

When do professional participants assume roles or undertake tasks that are outside of their province or beyond their expertise?

For example: When do judges act as psychiatrists by making their own psychological assessments of separating parents? When do social workers usurp the judicial role, either by withholding relevant information because they think the judge will "misuse" it or by slanting their reports to ensure that the judge will reach the "right" decision? When do child development specialists attempt to comply with requests by court or counsel rather than say "I'm not qualified to do what you ask"? When do court and counsel intrude upon the domain of an expert from another profession by insisting that he follow certain procedures which he considers unnecessary for the purpose of answering their questions? When do professional persons engage in unnecessary procedures in order to satisfy the demands of a participant from another discipline in the placement process?

When and under what circumstances are professionals who have acquired knowledge from another discipline justified in acting on such knowledge without expert assistance?

When does the assumption of two roles in relation to the same child or family place a professional beyond his competence, even though he is qualified to perform either role alone?

For example, does a social worker have the capacity to serve a child or family as *therapist* and at the same time, in relation to the same child or the same family, act as an *investigator* for a child care agency or family court?

When do professional participants act beyond their authority or professional knowledge by assuming the role of parents?

When, for example, do judges assume the parents' task of disciplining children, or lawyers assume the parents' role of deciding whether a child needs to consult a psychiatrist?

These questions do not fall into discrete units. We examine each separately in order to illustrate the many situations and multiple guises in which the problem of recognizing and respecting the boundaries of expert knowledge and the limits of professional authority may arise.

Chapter 2

❁

Untangling Professional and Personal Beliefs

It is not easy to separate personal values from professional knowledge and to distinguish both of these in turn from the societal values embedded in law. We learned and frequently had to remind ourselves of this while writing *Beyond the Best Interests of the Child* and *Before the Best Interests of the Child*.[1] Early on we became aware that most of our disagreements about conclusions were based neither upon our clinical experience nor upon any professional knowledge, but upon our personal values. We soon realized that we had failed to make these explicit to each other and often even to ourselves. And we had to learn to separate and hold in sharp focus the societal values reflected in the laws of child placement.

This experience made us realize the importance of informing our readers of the personal value preferences that we came to share. Consequently, in the opening chapters of *Beyond the Best Interests of the*

Child and of *Before the Best Interests of the Child,* we disclosed and discussed our preferences for a policy of *minimum state intervention* in parent–child relationships and for the policy of *making the child's interest paramount* once his care had become a legitimate matter for state intervention. We recognized that it was not solely our professional knowledge but our personal values which led us to assert that "the child's well-being—not the parents', the family's or the child care agency's—must be determinative once justification for state intervention has been established."[2] Thus we had to separate our personal commitment to children from our professional knowledge about child development and the status of children in law.[3]

We found it particularly difficult to untangle personal values from professional knowledge when both pointed in the same direction. As citizens, for instance, we favor the right of parents generally to raise their children free from government intrusion. As experts in child development, we recognize that the continuity of a child's relationships to his parents is vital to his health and therefore deserves the protection of the law. In other words, our views of government which underlie our personal preference for a policy of *minimum state intervention* are different from, though not in conflict with, our professional knowledge that a child needs to be wanted and in the uninterrupted day-to-day care of at least one person.

In this book we do not reopen questions addressed in the earlier volumes. Our concern is more with the practices of professional persons than with the substance of their recommendations or decisions.

Though our values remain the same, we have been careful not to let the force of our convictions and the temptation to reinforce the proposals we made in the earlier books lead us to find only good practices in decisions that we like and only poor practices in decisions we dislike. For example, though we recommended against coerced visitation in *Beyond the Best Interests of the Child*,[4] we identify good as well as poor professional practices in decisions that mandate visits and poor as well as good practices in decisions that refuse to order them.

We acknowledge another shared conviction. It is that the coercive power of the state ought not to be used to impose the dogma of one group on another in the name of science or other special knowledge.[5] When there is no societal consensus, the law should err on the side of protecting rights of parents to follow their own beliefs.

The task of untangling personal belief and professional knowledge is difficult even for a scientist. A United States Congressional Committee hearing on a bill to define when human life begins provides an example of good practice by a scientist and poor practice by the legislators. Dr. Leon Rosenberg, a geneticist, recognized that he was being pressed to answer a question outside of his scientific knowledge and said so. He drew a sharp distinction between his personal and his scientific beliefs:

> The crux . . . of the bill before you is the statement . . . "that present day scientific evidence indicates a significant likelihood that

actual human life exists from conception." I must respectfully but firmly disagree with this statement for two reasons: first, because I know of no scientific evidence which bears on the question of when actual human life exists; second, because I believe that the notion embodied in the phrase "actual human life" is not a scientific one, but rather a philosophic and religious one. . . .

. . . There is no reason to debate or to doubt the scientific evidence indicating that conception is a critical event in human reproduction. When the egg is fertilized by the sperm, a new cell is formed that contains all of the genetic information needed to develop ultimately into a human being. . . . But, in my view, there is an enormous difference between the *potential* for human life and, to repeat the critical phrase in Section 1 of this bill, "actual human life." To fulfill this potential, the fertilized egg must travel to the uterus, be implanted in the uterine wall, and undergo millions and millions of cell divisions leading to the development of its head, skeletal system, limbs and vital organs. To be sure, this sequence of events depends on the genetic program present in each cell of the developing embryo and fetus. As surely, however, the sequence depends on the environment offered by the mother. Without the genetic "blueprint" of the fetal cells, human development cannot be initiated; without the protection and nutrition provided by the mother's tissues, the genetic blueprint cannot be followed to completion. This absolute dependence of fetus on mother lasts normally for nine months, after which the birth process abruptly separates mother from child.

When does this potential for human life become actual? I do not know. Moreover, I have not been able to find a single piece of *scientific* evidence which helps me with that question. . . . I have no quarrel with anyone's ideas on this matter, so long as it is clearly understood that they are personal beliefs based on personal judgments, and not scientific truths.

If such beliefs are not scientific, you might say, just why can't they be made scientific? My answer is that science, per se, doesn't deal with the complex quality called "humanness" any more than it does with such equally complex concepts as love, faith, or trust. . . . I maintain that concepts such as humanness are beyond the purview of science because no idea about them can be tested experimentally. . . . If I am correct in asserting that the question of when actual life begins is not a scientific matter, then, you may ask, why have so many scientists come here to say that it is? My answer is that scientists, like all other people, have deeply held religious feelings to which they are entitled. In their remarks at these hearings, however, I believe that those who have preceded me have failed to distinguish between their moral or religious positions and their professional, scientific judgments.

* * *

Let me conclude by divesting myself of all scientific or clinical credentials and speak simply as an American. I believe we all know that this bill is about abortion and about nothing but abortion. If this matter is so compelling that our society cannot continue to accept a pluralistic view which makes women and couples responsible for their own reproductive decisions, then I say [ban] abortion. . . . But, don't ask science or medicine to help justify that course because they cannot. . . .[6]

Participants in the child placement process may find it even more difficult than geneticists to separate professional knowledge from personal belief. That is because in the child development field the boundaries between fact and value are harder to define. The focus of the geneticist, for example, is on the development of the fertilized egg into a child as it is protected and nurtured, subject to the *laws of nature,* in the relatively restricted confines of the *biochemical* environment of the mother's body. The focus of professionals in child placement is on the humanizing process—on the child's development into adulthood as he is protected and nurtured by his parents under the *laws of society,* in the relatively unrestricted confines of the *social* environment of which his family is part. In addition to sharing with the geneticist an interest in the physical well-being of children, the child development expert is concerned precisely with what Dr. Rosenberg calls "human-ness"—with the parent–child relationships after "the birth process separates mother from child"; with human qualities and needs such as affection, security, and trust. And the nature of the evidence upon which knowledge in child development and law rests—evidence concerned with the child's humanness—makes it difficult for experts who participate in the child placement process to locate the line that divides professional knowledge from ordinary knowledge.* Further, the legal standards for intervention and disposition provide professional participants with "no exact or even nearly exact scale of measurement like grams or ounces with which to balance. Personal prejudices are likely to creep into his [the judge's or counsel's] inexact measurings."[8] Another reason for the difficulty may be that all of the professional persons have been children, all have had parents, and many are themselves parents. Consequently, they have a multitude of personal beliefs and ordinary knowledge about what is best and bad for children

---

*We use "ordinary knowledge" as do Lindblom and Cohen, to "mean knowledge that does not owe its origin, testing, degree of verification, truth status, or currency to distinctive . . . professional techniques but rather to common sense, casual empiricism, or thoughtful speculation and analysis. It is highly fallible, but we shall call it knowledge even if it is false. As in the case of scientific knowledge, whether it is true or false, knowledge is knowledge to anyone who takes it as a basis for some commitment or action."[7]

and about what makes a good or unsatisfactory parent;[9] beliefs and knowledge which they, as adults moved by an urge to "rescue" children, are tempted to impose.* The risk that actions and decisions in child placement will rest on personal values presented in the guise of professional knowledge is therefore great—and all the more important to recognize.

Knowledge of professional persons who participate in the child placement process may go, in Rosenberg's words, "beyond the purview of [hard] science."† But such knowledge need not go beyond disciplined inquiry based upon clinical observations, written constitutions, statues, and case law.[12] Experience-based wisdom is often an integral part of special competence, but professionals must be alert not to use their reputations as experts to assume roles for which they have no special competence in furtherance of their personal values or of the preferences of those who engage their services.[13]

---

*"Everyone has ordinary knowledge—has it, uses it, offers it. It is not, however, a homogeneous commodity. Some ordinary knowledge, most people would say, is more reliable, more probably true, than other. People differ from each other in the kind and quality of ordinary knowledge they possess."[10]

†There may be a difference between "hard" and "soft" sciences, though the difference itself, upon close examination, may prove to be "soft" rather than "hard."[11]

Part Two

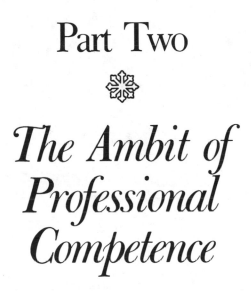

The Ambit of Professional Competence

Chapter 3

❁

Professional Boundaries

Boundaries between disciplines are not easily defined. Because professional persons bring to their work in the child placement process not only knowledge from their own discipline, but also a fund of ordinary knowledge, they sometimes make determinations that are not for them to make. While all professionals may be fact-finders, not all facts are for them to find. While all may be opinion givers, not all opinions are for them to give. "Am I qualified to find this fact or to give this opinion?" is a question all professional participants should ask themselves or be pressed to confront.

A JUDGE ACTING AS PSYCHOLOGIST WITH A SPECIALTY IN CHILD DEVELOPMENT AND AS EXPERT WITNESS—JASON ROSE

In *Rose v. Rose,* a divorce case, the task of the trial judge was to determine whether it would be in the best interest of two-and-one-half-year-old Jason to be placed in the custody of his mother, Diane, or to remain in the care of his father, Steven.[1] When Jason was six months old, his mother had attempted suicide by jumping from the eighth floor window of their apartment. Since that time Jason had been in his father's care. Following his mother's release after a six-month stay in the hospital, she had started to visit him.

The trial judge found that Diane, as well as Steven, was fit to care for Jason. Then, after observing that each parent had a "valid and reasonable claim" to custody, he said:

> Diane is still a bit immature, and certainly tending to excessive sarcasm, though I noticed this much less now than I did [at the hearing six months ago when I denied Diane custody while the divorce was pending]. Steve has progressed much faster academically than socially and emotionally....
>
> ... So, I come now to the part that's difficult too, for me, to really put into words. I'm going to give my impressions, because I think it's important for you all to know the basis for my judgments in this particular area. I have heard a great deal about Steve Rose from him and a great many witnesses, but I've also had the opportunity to watch him on the witness stand here, and down there at counsel table, for almost sixteen days now. It appears to me that he's a very demeaning person; he's prone to criticize and quick to demonstrate some kind of intellectual superiority. I got the impression

that he felt that he was smarter than a good
many of the experts who testified here. And in
considering the emotional makeup of the parties, the things they will pass on to their child,
and in subtle ways, I have given a large
preference here to Diane.

Accordingly, I find that the best interests of Jason lie in his care, custody, and control
by Diane Rose. . . .[2]

The judge assumed a professional role for
which he was not qualified. He acted as a psychologist
by using his own courtroom observations to determine the emotional makeup of Steven and Diane. As a
judge he was authorized to take into account his personal observations of the witnesses' behavior on the
stand for purposes of evaluating the veracity of their
testimony.[3] Here, however, he used these observations not for such an authorized purpose but to assess
the emotional and social maturity of two adults. He
assumed the role of expert in child development by
relating his findings about "the emotional makeup of
the parties" to "the things they will pass on to their
child . . . in subtle ways." Presumably deciding that
Steven would "pass on" detrimental traits to Jason,
he gave "a large preference" to Diane as the better
parent. He reached this conclusion despite guidance
from statutory and case law that "continuing an existing relationship and environment" is usually in the
child's best interest and despite uncontroverted expert evidence that Jason had thrived in Steven's
custody.[4]

The statutory presumption in favor of "continuing an existing relationship and environment" equipped the judge to resolve this custody dispute between two fit parents. He did not need, nor was he competent, to compare their personalities. A West Virginia court has observed: "[I]ntelligent determination of relative degrees of fitness requires a precision of measurement which is not possible given the tools available to judges."[5] In recognizing its own limitations, the court acknowledged that the law is a relatively crude instrument so far as specific individual relationships are concerned. As professionals, judges must recognize, and need not be embarrassed by, the limits of their knowledge. The West Virginia court stated: "Certainly it is no more reprehensible for judges to admit that they cannot measure gradations of psychological capacity between two fit parents than for a physicist to concede that it is impossible to measure the speed of an electron." Thus, except when the "facts demonstrate that care and custody were shared in an entirely equal way," the courts should determine custody in favor of whomever the facts establish as primary caregivers. Only when there are two primary caregivers (or no primary caregiver) must the court proceed "to inquire further into relative degrees of parental competence"[6]—or perhaps to draw lots if expert or other testimony offers no significant basis for choice.[7]

Had the judge in the *Rose* case realized that he was about to venture beyond what ordinary knowledge, his own training, the statutory guides or the testimony of the experts in the case qualified him to do, he might have acted differently. He might have asked counsel for both parties to present evidence on whether Steven's personality would be harmful to Jason's development and, if so, whether that harm would be greater than the harm that would result from uprooting the child and disrupting his relationship with his father. But the judge made his finding without explicitly posing such questions.* He thus denied himself the opportunity to learn from experts that they cannot make subtle comparisons between two fit parents and that they are unable to assess the relevance of a parent's "arrogance" or "immaturity" to a child's future well-being. Child development professionals might have (we maintain, *should* have) said "I don't know" in response to such questions. And they might have reinforced the statutory preference for maintaining the existing primary care relationship between a child and one of his parents by explaining that disruptions of ongoing relationships are likely to be harmful.†

*The issues we raise would be the same if the judge had decided to leave Jason in the custody of his father, not in order to safeguard "an existing relationship" but because he believed that Diane's "immaturity" would be more detrimental to Jason's interests than would Steven's "arrogance." See text following footnote 12, p. 27.

†The judicial process is meant to preclude the judge from resting his decision on his personal opinions—even opinions about matters, such as what makes a good parent, which he might have formed in his nonprofessional daily life. "There is," as Wigmore has observed, "a real but elusive line between the judge's *personal knowledge* as a private man and these matters of which he takes judicial notice as a judge. The latter does not necessarily include the former; as a judge, indeed, he may have to ignore what he knows as a man, and contrariwise."[8]

Even if the judge had been trained to make psychological assessments, he had no authority to become a witness, particularly one who did not take the stand.* By in effect receiving his own testimony—by being a covert witness—he denied Steven the opportunity to challenge his credentials as an expert. He also deprived Steven of the opportunity to introduce expert testimony which might have explained his "arrogant, overprotective, and critical behavior" as the response of an ordinary devoted parent who feared that his child's well-being was threatened. The judge might not have been persuaded by such testimony, but he should not have denied Steven's lawyer an opportunity to present it, or himself the obligation to consider it.

The judge was right, however, to disclose the extent to which his decision rested upon his personal observations. He said, "I think it's important for you all to know the basis for my judgments in this particular area."[9] He made visible a problem which may often go undisclosed and undiscovered. Thus, he provided a basis for an appeal to challenge his authority to be both judge and witness, his competence to make clinical psychological assessments, and the relevance of his comparison of parental fitness. Had these issues been perceived and raised, the appellate court might have reversed the trial court's judgment,[10] as did the Connecticut Supreme Court in another custody case:

*See Chapter 5.

In effect the trial [judge], as a basis for [his] findings, made of himself a witness, and in making [these findings] availed himself of his personal knowledge; he became an unsworn witness to material facts without the [parties] having any opportunity to cross-examine, to offer countervailing evidence or to know upon what evidence the decision would be made.[11]

Four years after ordering that Jason be placed in his mother's custody, the same trial judge, on the basis of expert testimony, granted Steven's petition that Jason be returned to his care. This time the judge explicitly recognized that his task was to weigh the harm Jason might suffer while in his mother's care against the "great weight" courts generally give to the benefits of staying with "the primary custodian."[12] But though the judge's *decision* to change custody was based on uncontradicted expert testimony, his *opinion* was again permeated with his own psychological observations. He recalled having rejected Steven as custodial parent because of his "arrogant, over-protective and super-critical attitude." He then implied that it was appropriate to have done so by explaining that while the father "appeared to retain some [of these traits] he has moderated" them and "has mellowed some in his previous poor attitudes. . . ." He then went on to suggest that Steven's improved attitude might be attributed to his remarriage. Moving further afield, he observed, "I assume [that Jason's slow rate of growth] will accelerate after a decision in this case, if it is somehow connected to something other than simply being the offspring of small parents. . . . I also assume that [Jason's] diagnosed depression, unhappiness and mood swings can be improved in time, given a better visitation schedule and more consistency in authority figures."[13] Possibly because the matter had not been addressed on the appeal from his first decision, the judge continued to act as if his law training and his appointment to the bench had qualified him to use his own observations to make psychological assessments and to determine their implications for a child's psychological and physical development.*

A JUDGE ACTING AS EXPERT IN CHILD DEVELOPMENT—Rachel Solomon

The custodial mother in *In re Marriage of Solomon* asked the court to order her former husband to reduce his visits with their daughter Rachel.[15] In response, the father requested that all parties submit to a psychiatric evaluation and that the judge order counseling for Rachel. The judge granted the request for an evaluation; he was guided by a statute which provided that a "court shall not restrict a parent's visitation rights unless it finds that the visitation would endanger seriously the child's . . . emotional

---

*If called upon to decide whether a child who is cross-eyed would be best served by corrective surgery, by a program of remedial exercises, or by the passage of time, a judge would undoubtedly recognize that he could not rely on his personal observations and experiences.[14]

health."[16] Following a two-month assessment which included eight sessions with the child, six with the father, two with the mother, and a consultation with a child psychologist, the psychiatrist, whose qualifications were accepted by both parties, testified that the child showed signs of extreme emotional tension, depression, impaired self-esteem, anxiety, and several abnormal personality traits and characteristics.[17] He recommended that Rachel receive psychological treatment. In response to the judge's question he said that it would be beneficial to alter the visitation pattern, but he testified that her problems did not arise from visitation "per se."

The judge then interviewed Rachel in chambers:

"Have you and your daddy been getting along?"

"I guess so."

"Do you like to see your daddy every week?"

"Yes."

"Do you love your daddy and mommy, do you—?"

"Yes."

In addition he asked her one question about her health, one about her participation in sports, one about her grades, and concluded: "She seems to be a very normal, nice little girl."[18] The mother testified that her daughter did not at any time suffer from anxiety, nervousness, or instability.

The judge granted the mother's request for a reduction of visits and denied the father's request for psychological treatment. He did not give the basis for either of these rulings.

The judge overstepped his competence when he reduced the father's visits. The statute authorized restrictions if visits would "endanger seriously the child's emotional health." Without the testimony of experts he would have remained unqualified to restrict visits under this provision of the statute. Therefore he had the authority—indeed the obligation—to order psychiatric evaluations, even over the mother's objection. Having heard the psychiatrist's uncontradicted testimony that Rachel's emotional health was not endangered by her father's visits—even if he did not find the testimony credible—it was beyond his authority and competence to restrict visits based on his own psychological evaluation of their impact.[19]

The judge may or may not have overstepped his competence when he refused to order treatment for Rachel. If he rested the denial on his conclusion, based on his interview, that Rachel was "very normal," he overstepped professional boundaries. His training did not qualify him to conduct diagnostic interviews or to make psychiatric assessments in order to determine whether there was a need for therapy. On the other hand, it was within his competence to refuse to order treatment either because he understood judicial and legislative policy to mean that only the mother, as custodial parent, had the right to consent to treatment for her daughter, or because he found the psychiatric testimony unpersuasive.*

The line is fine and difficult to draw between a judge who rules contrary to uncontradicted expert testimony because he relies on his own psychological assessments and a judge who does so because he does not believe or has not been persuaded by the expert. No more can be asked than that judges be sensitive to this concern and, like the judge in the *Rose* case, but unlike the judge in the *Solomon* case, make visible the basis of their rulings.

A LAWYER FOR THE CHILD ACTING AS MENTAL HEALTH EXPERT—LISA STONE

In *Stone v. Stone,* the divorced parents had agreed to a visitation schedule for their eight-year-old daughter Lisa. But visitation did not go smoothly. Lisa's mother, who had custody, claimed that the child was becoming increasingly reluctant to visit her father because of his verbal abuse and violent temper. Lisa's father insisted that her mind was being poisoned against him by the mother. The mother refused further visits and the father asked the court to order them. The judge was required by statute to apply the best interest standard in adjudicating disputes about

---

*We do not address here the merits of a policy which authorizes judges to supervene the judgment of parents about their child's medical care and to order, for example, psychiatric treatment. For our views on this issue see *Before the Best Interests of the Child*, Chapter 6.[20]

visits and to take into account the wishes of a child who "is old enough to form an intelligent preference." He appointed a lawyer to represent Lisa.

The lawyer spoke with Lisa, her teachers, and her doctor. He also heard complaints from each parent about the other's behavior and received several letters from Lisa describing in words and drawings her feelings of sadness and anger about having to visit her father. The lawyer reported to the court that visitations were "marked by confusion, discord, and sometimes violent and profane confrontations." Nevertheless, he recommended, on Lisa's behalf, that the court order visits. And he advised: "If it is true that Lisa is having such violent overreactions to visitations with her father, then it is certainly obvious that she is in dire need of professional counseling. It might be well for the court to order that all the parties concerned submit to sessions at the Family and Child Counseling Clinic."

The task of counsel for children is to discover and to represent the interests of the specific child who is their client.[21] There is no consensus as to the meaning of that task. Lisa's lawyer might have interpreted his assignment as limited to ascertaining and advocating her *expressed* preference—without seeking the advice of a child development expert to determine whether that was what she actually wanted. In that role he would have had to recommend that further visits not be ordered. Or he might have perceived his role as requiring him to advocate her *real* preference; he would then have needed expert assistance because:

[C] hildren of all ages have a natural tendency to deceive themselves about their motivations, to rationalize their actions, and to shy back from full awareness of their feelings, especially where conflicts of loyalty come into question. To pierce through these defenses demands more than usual skill from the investigator. Verbal and nonverbal communications (attitudes, behavior) have to be scrutinized, assessed, and translated into their underlying meaning; openings offered by the child, all unknowingly, have to be pursued and utilized. . . . The ability to make such contacts is demanded from psychiatric diagnosticians or child analysts as part of their professional equipment.[22]

A third possibility is that Lisa's lawyer might have perceived his role as an advocate not of her preference, expressed or real, but of her "best interest." In that event, too, he should have recognized the need to organize expert knowledge about the meaning of the visits for Lisa in order to equip the judge to make his decision. Lisa's lawyer might still have advocated that visits continue, but this time on the basis of an *informed* assessment.

No matter how Lisa's lawyer understood his appointment, he could not have understood it to include a request to render an opinion as to whether Lisa and her family were mentally ill or in need of treatment. If, in fact, he had been asked to do so, he would have realized that he was not qualified to make such evaluations or recommendations on his own.[23] Yet he allowed himself to slip into the role of expert in child development as well as adult psychiatry by characterizing Lisa's responses to the visits as "violent overreactions," by finding that she was "in dire need" of professional counseling, and by suggesting that the court order parents and child to "submit to" therapy.

Lisa's lawyer failed to ask,"Am I qualified to determine on my own that continued visits are in the best interests of Lisa?" He did not provide expert testimony upon which the judge could rely. Nor did he recognize that as a lawyer he was not qualified to evaluate the mental health of Lisa and her parents, and that he exceeded his assignment as well as his competence when he prescribed therapy for them.*[24]

A SOCIAL WORKER ACTING AS EXPERT IN CHILD DEVELOPMENT—Maria Colwell

Social work training and experience are not as far removed from training in child development as are legal training and experience. Social workers may therefore find it even more difficult than judges and lawyers to recognize and stay within their profes-

---

*Perhaps Lisa's lawyer was in a bind. He may have had no resources and little time and he might have understood that a finding of "best interest" required him to assess "psychological issues." Under such circumstances he should have said to the judge who appointed him, "I'm not qualified to determine the meaning of Lisa's violent reactions. The court must appoint a psychiatrist to inform me."

sional boundaries when evaluating the behavior of children.[25] The *Report of the Commission of Inquiry into the Death of Maria Colwell** was critical of a social worker for relying on her own assessment of Maria's behavior (without consulting a child development expert) when Maria was made to leave her foster parents and visit her natural mother and stepfather:

> ... The social worker's view of Maria's distress and resistance may be summed up succinctly as (1) being due to her fear of losing [her foster parents] rather than any fear or dislike of [her natural mother and stepfather], and (2) that in any event it was within expected and well recognised limits in such circumstances. Nor was [the social worker] prepared to admit at the Inquiry that the independent views of a medical man such as a psychiatrist ... could have added anything to the picture that would have assisted her, and presumably this was also her senior officer's opinion. ... [The social worker] said that because of the tensions in the situation she had to make an intelligent guess as to Maria's true feelings. We were also told that ... scenes ... are quite common when this sort of "transfer of loyalties"—as it was described—is being attempted. While we accept that a certain amount of distress may be unavoidable, we can-

*Maria, a seven-year-old girl, had been beaten to death by her stepfather shortly after the court ordered her to be returned to the care of her natural mother.

not accept that in a case such as this a child should be subjected to the degree of stress shown by Maria. Nor do we consider an intelligent guess as to the cause of that stress to be sufficient in this case.

We find it difficult to understand why [the social worker] took the view she did about seeking psychiatric or paediatric advice at this time. We appreciate that social work training contains an element of child psychology. Surely, however, such training should enable social workers to turn readily for specialist help when severe trauma presents, so that medical skill can supplement their own casework skill.

* * *

... To our mind, there was never at any time upon the evidence before us, any doubt at all where Maria's loyalties lay, and that was with the [foster parents]. On that ground the report can be criticised, but it is important to realise that this only arises because of the social workers' assumptions about the trauma, which we have already indicated they were not qualified to make on their own in the particular circumstance of this case. . . .[26]

The Commission of Inquiry had the benefit of hindsight. Because the social worker's training included "an element of child psychology" and because in her work for the local authority she had probably observed other children who cried bitterly when they were separated from their foster parents, yet seemed to make a good adjustment to the move, she concluded that Maria's kicking and screaming was "within expected and well recognised limits in such circumstances," and decided not to oppose the natural mother's petition to have Maria returned to her permanently.

Had Maria not been murdered, it is probable that no inquiry would have occurred and that the social worker's failure to consult an expert in child development would not have come to light. The activities of professional participants in the child placement process are often of low visibility. This covert quality increases the importance of their recognizing the borders of their own area of expertise and remaining within them—not an easy task.*

CHILD DEVELOPMENT PROFESSIONALS RECOGNIZING THE LIMITS OF THEIR EXPERTISE

IN A PUBLIC INTEREST LAWSUIT

At the request of two public interest lawyers, Dr. Maynard, a nationally recognized child psychoanalyst, prepared an affidavit explaining why, from a foster child's point of view, the state should establish procedures to protect long-term relationships be-

*In the U.S.A. many social workers have had academic and clinical training in child development sufficient to make informed judgments about a child's behavior and feelings. The challenge for them as well as for other professionals is to recognize when there is a need for consultation with other experts.

tween these children and their caregivers. The lawyers intended to use the affidavit in a class action suit
to reform the foster care system. They later asked Dr.
Maynard to prepare an additional affidavit in support
of their claim that they could represent, as a single
class, not only foster children, but also their natural
parents and their foster parents. He said:

> I don't understand what you want.

They explained that in this suit all three groups
had a common, nonconflicting, interest in the pro-
cedural reforms:

> An affidavit from you would lend support to
> our view that the reforms we propose would be
> beneficial to all concerned. You can persuade
> the court that the three groups can be treated
> as a single class whom we can represent
> without conflict.

Dr. Maynard refused their request. He said:

> I was qualified to say what I said in the first af-
> fidavit and to support your efforts on behalf of
> foster children. But I know I'm not qualified to
> say that what is beneficial for the children is
> beneficial for the competing adults.

The lawyers said:

> We don't understand. You are a distinguished
> figure whose prestige can be used to endorse

our legal strategy for achieving goals which you, as a child development expert, already support.

Dr. Maynard replied:

I don't want you to use my professional reputation to decorate your case. Let me tell you, I don't find it easy to resist the temptation to lend my name to support a cause I believe in. And I enjoy being asked for my opinion in cases that will receive nationwide attention. But I always have to ask myself, and particularly when I'm feeling flattered, "Am I being urged to lend my reputation to an opinion which I cannot substantiate on the basis of my professional knowledge and experience?"

Dr. Maynard's observation, like the testimony of Dr. Rosenberg before the Congressional Committee,[27] illustrates how professional persons can be alert to recognize when they are being urged to answer questions on the basis of personal values rather than professional knowledge.

IN AN ADOPTION
CASE—Mario and Fidel Chavez

Two child development experts, Dr. Blanchard and Dr. Abel, were engaged by Tom Smith, lawyer for Mr. and Mrs. Walter Wright, to advise him "whether it would be best for the two Chavez children—Mario (10 years) and Fidel (7 years)—to remain with and be adopted by the Wrights or to be returned to their natural mother." Attorney Smith said that he hoped their report could establish that the Wrights were the psychological parents of the Chavez boys. But he added that what his clients wanted most to know was whether adoption by them would be in the best interests of Mario and Fidel. Unlike the lawyers in the class action suit, Smith did not press the experts to reach a particular result or to use their reputations to support claims that were beyond their professional expertise. And the experts, sensitive to the limits of their professional knowledge and conscious of the borders between their discipline and that of lawyers and judges, wrote the following report:

> This is our assessment of Mario and Fidel Chavez, who are presently residing with Mr. and Mrs. Walter Wright.
> After interviews with Mr. and Mrs. Wright, the two boys and Mr. and Mrs. Alberto Diaz,[*] and after psychological examination by Dr. Robin Rhodes, we have formed an opinion in response to your request that we advise you about whether it would be best for Mario and Fidel to remain permanently in the custody of the Wrights or to be returned to their natural mother, Mrs. Diaz:
> In May 1979 the boys, then living with their mother in El Salvador, were placed by her in the custody of Mr. and Mrs. Wright with the

[*] The boys' natural mother and her new husband.

understanding that they would take them to America and adopt them. Together with the Wrights, Mario and Fidel arrived in the United States in June 1979 and were immediately placed in the home of Mrs. Wright's married sister in Connecticut. The Wrights (who had been living and working in El Salvador for many years) began their search for employment and a home in Massachusetts. They spent weekends with Mario and Fidel until March 1980 when they found employment and purchased a home in Springfield, Massachusetts. Then, with the assistance of a housekeeper, they assumed direct responsibility for the care of Mario and Fidel, who are now living with them. For a period of 15 days in November 1980, the boys were separated from the Wrights. They had been flown to Florida by their mother and Mr. Diaz without the Wrights' prior knowledge or permission.[*]

Because of the almost eighteen months separation from their mother and because of the instability and frequently changing custodial arrangements for their care since arriving in the United States, as well as the insecurity accompanying the litigation over their custody, Mario and Fidel do not at present have primary psychological ties to any adult.

---

[*]Mrs. Chavez had managed to enter the United States and shortly thereafter in January 1980 she married Alberto Diaz, a United States citizen.

We find that the boys' attachment to the Wrights is not yet a primary psychological relationship. It might best be characterized by calling it a friendship growing out of less than two years of continuous and direct custody. The children are comfortable in their present setting. Similarly, the boys do not at present have a primary psychological relationship to Mrs. Diaz. It may best be characterized as a substantial but residual tie damaged by the long separation and by the exigencies of growing up in a war-torn country. As a result of events outside of the control of any of the interested parties, the capacity of the children to make firm attachments has been impaired. They do not sense themselves as members of any family and look with anxiety upon any change. Thus, the assignment of custody cannot be based on an assumption that one adult has a more basic psychological and emotional relationship to these children than the other adult. In addition to a common language and cultural heritage Mrs. Diaz, of course, has a longer period of experiential contacts, as well as the earliest continuous relationship that preceded and in turn is associated with deprivation and disruption.

The children's psychological tests and their good school performance reflect emotional and intellectual strengths from the past, as well as the nurturing environment in which they now live. An uninterrupted opportunity to establish primary psychological ties to someone they come to know as parent(s) offers the only real chance these children have to meet the difficulties of the developmental tasks that lie ahead.

The Wrights have a strong wish to provide and are providing affectionate care for these children. Mrs. Diaz has demonstrated her affection for the boys and evidenced great tenacity and ingenuity in safeguarding them until they left El Salvador and in seeking to reconstitute her family. Mr. Diaz seems to fully support his wife's efforts. We do not question the qualifications of either the Wrights to adopt or of Mrs. Diaz to resume her role as parent.

Our knowledge does not enable us to make long-term predictions about which placement might be best. For the long-term benefit of these children what remains critical is that doubt and uncertainty about their placement end as quickly as possible in making one of these choices permanent. Whatever the court decides, these children need to know that the court's decision is a permanent one. These children yearn for permanency.

It is clear that it would be corrosive and damaging to the children if the court were to postpone a final decision in the false hope that further investigation could produce what only hindsight may ultimately reveal.

When the psychological reasons for making a choice between two available alternatives are substantially in balance, the one remaining critical factor for the long-term benefit of the children is that the choice be made quickly and unconditionally and that the uncertainty and doubt about whom they belong to be removed.

Dr. Abel testified as an expert witness at the court hearing. At the conclusion of his testimony, which was practically identical to the written report, the trial judge turned to him and said, "Now doctor, between us, tell me who do you really think would make the better parents?" Dr. Abel replied, "I can't answer that question, Your Honor," and thought to himself, "The judge is pressing me to step outside of my professional role. I do know which set of parents I personally would prefer, but my preference rests, not on my professional knowledge, but on my middle-class notions of the 'good life.' I would be abusing my professional responsibility were I to disclose my personal opinion to the judge."

In both their report and testimony these experts were careful not to draw conclusions that went beyond their professional knowledge.[28]

WORKING TOGETHER—JUDGE ACTING AS A JUDGE, LAWYER ACTING AS A LAWYER, AND CHILD DEVELOPMENT EXPERT ACTING AS A CHILD DEVELOPMENT EXPERT

Whoever represents the child and whoever determines his placement must decide whether to obtain and how to use knowledge of the developmental needs of children. Joyce and James Robertson describe one way in which experts might provide such knowledge—by serving not only as witnesses but also as advisors to the child's legal representatives throughout a court hearing. Their account of a foster care case illustrates how participants from different disciplines can effectively interact and prevent each other from straying unnoticed beyond their professional borders.

> A child has been with foster parents from [the age of] 6 months to [the age of] 4 years, placed there by the local authority because of the mother's unfitness to look after her. Mother and stepfather took a dislike to the foster parents and sought to have the child moved elsewhere. The local authority, although they had no complaint against the foster parents but were under [severe] pressure, decided to effect the change. The foster parents challenged this decision. . . . The authority put the child aged 4 years into the "neutral situation"[*] of a

[*] "There is no neutral situation for a young child parted from those she loves. Feelings and needs do not go into suspension. That this child was removed from adequate substitute parents indicates failure to recognize that she was emotionally a child of the foster parents, with the certainty of acute distress and probably damage through being separated from them.

"The inescapable fact is that once a young child leaves the care of his family, however necessary that may be, he is emotionally at risk because of the rupture of his relationships. These will be broken again if, in due course, he has to give up a temporary caretaker to whom he has become attached, even to return to the mother. If leaving his family subjects him to a succession of caretakers the risk to his emotional health are compounded."[29]

children's home pending the decision of the court, and the child had been there for 4 months.

There were therefore four parties to the hearing, each represented by counsel:

1. The mother and the stepfather seeking to have the child removed from the long-term foster home to another.
2. The local authority, proposing to make the move.
3. The foster parents, resisting the move on grounds that it was against the interests of the child who was as if of their family.
4. The 4-year-old child, legally represented by a *guardian ad litem* who had . . . [recommended that] the judge . . . accept the local authority's proposal to remove the child from her foster family.

[We] appeared as expert witnesses on behalf of the foster parents. We considered that the foster parents' plea was in the best interest of the child. But we would have preferred to have been standing behind the *guardian ad litem* [appointed by the state] instead of one of the contending parties.

After giving evidence, we did not leave the court but, with the judge's permission, stayed throughout the hearing. . . . It was then that we realised the disadvantage to the young child of having only legal representation. Each of the other parties sat behind their counsel, and as evidence was led they could offer comment and correction which their counsel could use. But the child was not in court, and there was no one to tug at her counsel's sleeve;[*] and of course he was not equipped to perceive matters through the eyes of a child.

At various points where it seemed to us that the *guardian ad litem* was not reacting with knowledge of child development, we passed notes down to the foster parents' counsel and he used these effectively in interventions—technically in the foster parents' interests, but from our view ensuring that the status of the child was better understood.[31]

The judge utilized the Robertsons' presence to help him recognize when persons strayed into areas outside their competence. In this hearing, unlike that in Jason's case, the "unprofessional" interpretation of facts did not go unchallenged:

Several witnesses were brought by the opposing sides to discredit the foster parents. For instance, a staff member from the children's home described the child as attention-seeking and having temper tantrums. These were proper observations, but when asked to do so she gave [her] opinion that the behavior in-

[*]Even if the child were in court, her counsel might still have required someone with knowledge of child development to "tug at his sleeve" and to correct misreadings of her conduct.[30]

dicated that the child had been badly reared by the foster parents.

We passed a note to our counsel saying that the behavior was typical of a young child separated from those she loved and placed in an institution. Counsel immediately used this information and the judge agreed that the witness was being led to make judgments which were outside his competence. . . . Again, a domestic gave evidence of emotional behavior in the [foster] mother said to indicate instability. . . . We passed a note saying that the foster mother was behaving appropriately for a woman under the great stress of having been deprived of a de facto daughter. This too was accepted by the court.

These two examples illustrate the very important point that because the *guardian ad litem* had only legal knowledge, those misinterpretations of the behavior of child and foster mother might have gone unchallenged and have weighed against the foster mother.[32]

The Robertsons conclude:

Although we had remained as observers only, we gradually found that we were being used by the court and brought into consultation by the judge. He was aware of the ongoing guidance we were giving to the foster parents' counsel, and in further sessions in the witness box he [sought clarification of the concept of] "psychological parent" and [its] implications for this child's best interests.

After some days the counsel for the local authority and the *guardian ad litem* withdrew their submissions in explicit acceptance of the Robertson evidence. The judge then ordered that the child be returned to the foster parents, and in his summing up acknowledged his indebtedness to the guidance on emotional development given by the Robertsons.

The point of all this is that the court needed access to specialized knowledge of child development throughout the hearing, and that as the child had been given only legal representation this psychological knowledge would not have been available had we not remained in court.[33]

The problem is not, as the Robertsons suggest, that the *guardian ad litem* gave the child *only* legal representation, but that he did not give the child *full* legal representation. He failed to recognize that he did not know enough about child development and parent-child relationships to know whether to accept or to challenge the witnesses' interpretations of the behavior of the child and her primary caregivers.

Lawyers and judges abdicate their professional roles when they allow a court hearing to be limited to rubber stamping (or, for that matter, to rejecting automatically) proposals made by child welfare agencies or local authorities. One of the arguments for providing a child with independent counsel in such cases is that the state cannot be presumed to represent the interests of the particular child.* That argument rests on the not always realistic expectation that judges conduct hearings in order to learn enough to make informed decisions. Judge Breitel has observed:

> In custody matters parties and courts may be very dependent on the auxiliary services of psychiatrists, psychologists, and trained social workers. This is good. But it may be an evil when the dependence is too obsequious or routine or the experts too casual. Particularly important is this caution where one or both parties may not have the means to retain their own experts and where publicly compensated experts or experts compensated by only one side have uncurbed leave to express opinions which may be subjective or not narrowly controlled by the underlying facts.[35]

At the court hearing in which the Robertsons testified, counsel for the foster parents never lost sight of the purpose of the hearing. He challenged the position of witnesses for the local authority, even though he might have predicted that his client would lose. He recognized what may too often go unrecognized: The judge had a choice to make, and even if

*As we have said elsewhere, "Even child care agencies which are delegated responsibility for safeguarding the welfare of children often have conflicts of interest between their need to safeguard some agency policy and the needs of the specific child to be placed."[34]

lawyers can reasonably predict on the basis of past decisions that the court will rule against what they consider the child's interest, they must prepare for and insist upon a full hearing.

It is true that lawyers are equipped by training and experience to predict the outcome of a case. They serve their clients well, for example, in a contract or even in a criminal case if they consider with them the costs of continued litigation as well as the benefits of prevailing. Even when they believe that right (as recognized by case law or statute) is on their side, they may advise their clients to settle, to drop the claim, or to bargain a plea. But when the well-being of a child is at stake, they do a disservice to him if they *use* their predictions to deny the trial judge or the appellate court a choice by withdrawing the claim on behalf of the child, or by not presenting every shred of evidence that they can gather to enable the judge to decide differently than predicted. Such predictions cannot justify the failure to uncover and present information which might cast doubt on the wisdom of the expected outcome.*

Counsel for the foster parents recognized the limitations of his and the judge's knowledge of child development. He did what lawyers do in almost any other kind of case. He utilized experts to interpret facts or to question the interpretation of facts by others—including the judge—who were ill-equipped to do so without expert guidance.[36] Aided by the child

---

*The problem of lawyers' using prediction of outcome in child placement cases is examined in Chapter 4, pp. 74–78 *infra.*

development experts during the hearing, counsel was able to demonstrate that crucial testimony by local authority witnesses was beyond their competence. By challenging the position of the local authority and by organizing and presenting relevant information to the judge, counsel for the foster parents gave full legal representation to his clients and in this case also the child, since their interests coincided.

The *guardian ad litem,* on the other hand, failed to introduce independent expert testimony either to support or to challenge the local authority's position. He accepted, without question, eye-witness testimony about the behavior and the meaning of the behavior of foster mother and child. The *guardian ad litem* would, no doubt, have perceived the need for expert testimony in a case concerning a building, not a child. Were the collapse of a walkway in a hotel a matter of legal concern, he would have recognized his own and the judge's need to be educated by experts in structural design. Such education would be needed to qualify them to determine whether the internal structural failures were caused by external stresses and could have been prevented. No lawyer or judge would accept unquestioningly the testimony of nonexpert eyewitnesses on the cause of the collapse.

Where human behavior is at issue, the need for experts to inform the judge as to its meaning and implications is less easily recognized than when the "behavior" of nonhuman structures is involved.[37] This blind spot, which may result in less than full legal representation of the child's interests in placement cases, seems to stem from two different and conflicting attitudes. One attitude, shared by professional participants, particularly by lawyers and judges, is that human relationships are so complex that a court hearing cannot educate a judge sufficiently to make a decision. Therefore judges and lawyers should simply defer to child care agencies. The other attitude is that human relationships are so much a part of ordinary knowledge that there is no need for experts to assess the conduct of a particular child or his caregivers.[38]

The Robertsons' case demonstrates what seems to be easily forgotten, especially when one of the parties is a state agency or local authority "acting on behalf of the child." It is that the function of a court hearing is to equip the judge to make an informed decision about a matter that he would otherwise be unqualified to decide. A child is put at unnecessary risk when his legal representatives assume that they "know" the child's needs, or that they "know" the decision the judge will make. A child is put at unnecessary risk when his legal representatives do not think about whether they need to engage child development experts to enable them, and in turn, the judge, to make informed assessments of the facts when considered through the eyes of a child. A child is put at unnecessary risk when a judge assumes that he has no choice but to accept the proposal of a child care authority and does not use the hearing to educate himself sufficiently to determine whether his decision is indeed in the child's best interest.

[handwritten margin note: reasons for insufficient representation of child's interests]

Chapter 4

Crossing Professional Borders

In the preceding chapter we emphasized the importance of assuring that professional persons acknowledge and act within the ambit of their disciplines. In this chapter, while continuing to recognize the separateness of the different disciplines, we want to emphasize that they cannot and need not be rigidly compartmentalized. Indeed, the effectiveness of participation by persons of different disciplines in the child placement process depends on their learning from one another. A workable child placement process will provide for a conscious, restrained, open, and reviewable use by professional participants of knowledge acquired from a discipline not their own. The art of collaboration grows out of a recognition that borders do exist, even if they cannot always be sharply defined, and that under certain circumstances they may be crossed.

54

By working together and reading each others' writings, professional participants in the child placement process may acquire some special knowledge from another discipline. For example, from their work with child development experts, family court judges and child advocates may learn that the custody of a child who has thrived in long-term care with the same foster family cannot be changed without harming him. From collaboration with agency lawyers and through attending court hearings, social workers may learn that certain judges usually deny petitions to free a battered child for permanent placement, though they will grant petitions for temporary custody. From testifying in custody cases and from reading court opinions, experts in child development may learn that their reports are not likely to be given credence if they fail to interview and psychologically test each child and adult involved—even when they believe that they have enough information to respond to the judge's questions without such tests.

Learning by experience—from child development for the law trained and from law for the nonlaw trained—does not necessarily justify these professional persons acting on what they have learned. Their knowledge of another discipline may be no longer valid. Or their acquired knowledge may be valid but not necessarily applicable to a particular case. And even valid, generally applicable knowledge from another discipline should be acted on only if doing so will not contravene the dictates of the participant's own professional training.

The cases that follow illustrate the kind of questions professional persons should address in deciding whether to cross boundaries—whether to act on their acquired knowledge.

LAW TRAINED PROFESSIONALS USING THEIR KNOWLEDGE OF CHILD DEVELOPMENT

LAWYER AND JUDGE

In *Rivera v. Marcus,* a U.S. District Court held that a foster mother's constitutional rights had been violated when, seven years earlier, two children were removed from her care without due process.[1] The usual remedy in such cases is an order to return the children.[2] But the court, at the request of counsel for the children, did not automatically issue the order. Counsel advised the court that taking the children from their present foster family might be detrimental to them. On the basis of knowledge acquired by working with child psychiatrists and by studying the literature of child development, he was alert to the risk involved for these children. He advised the court that "the stability of [their] current situation and their bonds to their present foster parents should be carefully considered before uprooting them."[3] By agreeing to hold a hearing, the District Court judge demonstrated that he knew enough about a child's need for continuity of care not to move these children until he had heard expert testimony on the potential effect of such a move.

The children's lawyer and the District Court

judge properly crossed professional borders. Their reliance on knowledge from child development was visible and open to challenge and did not conflict with or undermine their own professional roles. The lawyer did not cease to act as advocate for his clients and the judge did not abdicate his judicial function.[4]

COURTS

In *Ross v. Hoffman,* the chancellor of a Maryland equity court decided to leave Melinda Ross, age 9, in the custody of Mr. and Mrs. Hoffman, her long-term foster parents. Mrs. Ross, Melinda's mother, argued that the Hoffmans had failed to overcome the presumption in law "that a child's welfare will be best served in the custody of the natural parents." She asserted that the chancellor erroneously relied upon the theory of "psychological parenthood" from *Beyond the Best Interests of the Child.*[5] The chancellor had said:

> [In] that book [the authors] point out that whether any adult becomes a psychological parent over the child is based upon a day-to-day interaction, companionship and shared experiences. And if you look at it from that view, Mrs. Hoffman ... was the day-to-day person while Mrs. Ross ... would go once or twice a week, ... and there were ... long periods of absences, and they say this role can be fulfilled by ... any other caring adult, ... whatever the relationship may be. ...
>   Further, there is something I use ...

from the Family Law Report on Child Custody Conciliation. . . . They talk about mothering the young child. They said the word "mothering" denot[es] *function* rather than a person. The function does not reside in the biological mother. . . .

* * *

It is the adults within the home of the child . . . with whom the child can interact meaningfully, . . . and I think that is what [the child psychiatrist] had in mind [when he said] why risk [moving Melinda] because we know what this child can do in the home of the Hoffmans. She is well-developed and healthy, and if we change the custody we are not sure whether Mrs. Ross and her new husband and this child can interact meaningfully with her.[6]

On the basis of his acquired knowledge, buttressed by expert testimony applied to undisputed facts, the chancellor had recognized that the presumption in favor of Mrs. Ross as natural parent had been overcome.* For him to have applied that presumption in

*In this case, the two sources of information on which the judge relied—"acquired knowledge" and "expert testimony"— happened to agree. But what if there is a conflict between, for example, what the judge has learned from reading and what he hears from an expert testifying at the trial? No more can be asked than that the judge articulate the basis of his finding, so that it can be reviewed and called into question during the hearing or on appeal by experts of the same or different schools of thought or even different disciplines.[7]

this case would have defeated its function. As a New York court has observed, that function is to safeguard the "security, continuity and 'long term stability'. . . [that] are vital to the successful personality development of a child" and that biological parents usually provide.[8]

An intermediate appellate court emphasized the importance of the chancellor having made visible the basis for his decision and thus leaving it open to challenge and review: "[He] reviewed at great length the facts and testimony upon which he relied [and] explained that his reasoning had, to some extent, been influenced by certain educational background factors to which he had been exposed extra-judicially. . . ."[9] The court acknowledged that the boundaries between disciplines may sometimes be crossed:

> To expect [a] judge . . . to erase from memory all that he has read or experienced, not specifically related to the facts of a case, before deciding a case is an absurdity so apparent as to deserve no rebuttal. Error would result when the reasoning was obviously distorted, but not when sound reasoning is influenced by prior experience or education. The soundness of the chancellor's reasoning here is apparent from the excerpt of his opinion. We do not find that he gave undue weight to that particular underpinning of his reasoning. Rather, we commend him both for recognizing and expressing that which helped him to decide.[10]

The Maryland Supreme Court affirmed the intermediate appellate court's decision. Its opinion reflects the way in which expert knowledge—here about a child's need for continuity—can gradually enter case law and in a limited way, as precedent, become a part of the professional equipment of judges and lawyers. The precedent established in *Ross v. Hoffman* incorporates generally accepted and generally applicable knowledge from the field of child development. These precedents, in some cases, enable lawyers to argue against and qualify courts to overturn, without hearing expert testimony, the presumption in favor of natural parents. Lawyers and judges on their own can come to recognize many "parent"-child relationships that should normally not be disturbed. Thus, through judicial precedent the borders between the professions are opened and may legitimately be crossed under certain circumstances.

The Maryland Supreme Court made several general observations reflecting its understanding of the knowledge it had acquired. It said:

> The child may be so long in the custody of the nonparent that, even though there had been no [legal] abandonment or persistent neglect by the parent, the psychological trauma of removal is grave enough to be detrimental to the best interest of the child. . . . "Changes in conditions which affect the relative desirability of custodians . . . are not to be accorded significance unless the advantages of changing cus-

tody outweigh the essential principle of continued and stable custody of children."[11]

The court then listed specific criteria for determining
whether someone other than the natural parent is the
child's primary caregiver and should have custody of
the child:

> The factors which emerge from our prior deci-
> sions which may be of probative value . . . in-
> clude the length of time the child has been away
> from the biological parent, the age of the child
> when care was assumed by the third party, the
> possible emotional effect on the child of a
> change of custody, the period of time which
> elapsed before the parent sought to reclaim the
> child, the nature and strength of the ties be-
> tween the child and the third party custodian,
> the intensity and genuineness of the parent's
> desire to have the child, the stability and cer-
> tainty as to the child's future in the custody of
> the parent.
>
> *   *   *
>
> [Here practically all criteria were present.] His
> conclusion, that custody in the Hoffmans was
> in the child's best interests, was founded upon
> sound legal principles. . . .[12]

The intermediate appellate court itself had recognized the limits of its acquired knowledge. It cau-

tioned that the knowledge of judges was insufficient to "fix a period for which a parent may [cast] off the robe of parental responsibility both inwardly and outwardly, before forfeiting the judicially espoused presumptive shield provided a natural parent."[13]

LEGISLATURE

Special knowledge from child development can also enter the law by legislation. For example, in abolishing the maternal preference,* the Oregon legislature incorporated knowledge from child development in listing these factors to be considered in determining custody:

(a) The emotional ties between the child and other family members;
(b) the interest of the parties in and attitude toward the child; and
(c) the desirability of continuing an existing relationship.[14]

Knowledge from child development is similarly reflected in those factors which the legislature listed as only secondarily relevant:

In determining custody of a minor child . . . the court shall consider the conduct, marital status, income, social environment or life style of either party *only* if it is shown that any of

*The maternal preference is a presumption that children, particularly of tender years, should remain in the custody of their mother.

these factors are causing or may cause emotional or physical damage to the child.[15]

In applying these statutory guidelines, the Oregon Supreme Court in *Derby v. Derby* recognized the significance of identifying the primary caretaking (or, more properly, caregiving)* parent regardless of gender:

> The undisputed evidence in this case was that the wife was not merely the mother, but was also the primary parent. During the marriage she was not working and performed the traditional and honorable role of homemaker. She cleaned the house, cared for the children, fed the family, nursed them when sick and spent those countless hours disciplining, counseling and chatting with the children that every homemaker should. For some families the husband may perform this role and be the primary parent. . . . In this family [he] played the traditional role of breadwinner, working eight to ten hours a day. In his off-hours he dedicated much time and attention to the children, but the lion's share of the child raising was performed by the wife. It is undisputed that the children were happy and well-adjusted and that the relationship between the wife and the children was

---

*We prefer "caregiving" to "caretaking" because it more accurately reflects the human nature of the parent–child relationship.

> close, loving and successful. Although the same relationship unquestionably existed to a degree with the husband, the close and successful emotional relationship between the primary parent and the children coupled with the age of the children dictate the continuance of that relationship.[16]

In Oregon, lawyers and judges thus no longer need expert testimony in every divorce-custody case before determining who is the child's primary caregiver.[17] As with judicial precedent, in a limited way and for a limited purpose, special knowledge from child development has become part of the working knowledge of the law trained participants.[18] This acquired knowledge is, of course, highly visible and remains open to review and challenge in specific cases as well as generally by legislative revision.

COURT AND LEGISLATURE

The Supreme Court of West Virginia has interpreted its legislature's decision to abolish "all gender based presumptions" for awarding custody to mean that a child's "primary caretaker parent" should be preferred. West Virginia's statute provided only that custody awards accord with "the best interest of the child."[19] Unlike the Oregon statute, it contained no guidelines for identifying the parent who would best serve the child. This lack of guidelines forced the court to analyze its reasons for having adopted the now-prohibited maternal preference. In *Garska v. Mc-Coy*, it found that the preference had been designed to assure that the parent, who through caretaking was "closest to the child" would be given custody. The West Virginia court turned to the child development-based legislative and judicial decisions of Oregon for guidance in establishing factors for deciding custody:

[The] trial court shall determine which parent has taken primary responsibility for, *inter alia*, the performance of the following caring and nurturing duties of a parent:

(1) preparing and planning of meals;

(2) bathing, grooming, and dressing;

(3) purchasing, cleaning, and care of clothes;

(4) medical care, including nursing and trips to physicians;

(5) arranging for social interaction among peers after school; i.e., transporting to friends' houses or, for example, to girl or boy scout meetings;

(6) arranging alternative care, i.e., babysitting, daycare, etc.;

(7) putting child to bed at night, attending to child in the middle of the night, waking child in the morning;

(8) disciplining, i.e., teaching general manners and toilet training;

(9) educating, i.e., religious, cultural, social, etc.; and,

(10) teaching elementary skills, i.e., reading, writing, and arithmetic.[*][20]

The court went on to explain the relationship between these factors and the need of children for continuity of care. Taking into account child development considerations practically identical to those reflected in the Oregon statute, the court said:

> While, as the trial court found, the educational and economic position of the father is superior to that of the mother, nonetheless, those factors alone pale in comparison to love, affection, concern, tolerance, and the willingness to sacrifice—factors about which conclusions can be made for the future most intelligently upon a course of conduct in the past. At least with regard to the primary caretaker parent there is a track record to which a court can look and where that parent is fit he or she should be awarded continued custody.[21]

Whether established by statute, as in Oregon, or by judicial precedent, as in West Virginia, the primary caretaker guidelines explicitly identify the factors to be considered in terms of their func-

---

[*]These indicia of the primary caregiver, like those listed in *Derby v. Derby,* may or may not be acceptable to experts in child development or generally applicable in this or other cultural settings. What matters is that they, and indeed the primary caregiving preference itself, are open to review, to challenge, and to change.

tion—assuring continuity of care for the child. They enable judges and lawyers to achieve a degree of literacy in child development—to gain some understanding of the reasons for the preference. Unlike the earlier preferences for the mother or for biological parents, the preference for the primary caregiving parent provides more than "mere assertions of end results."[22] The new preference is no longer divorced from the ideas, concepts, and theories that need to be understood in order to recognize its purpose. The gender-related, the blood-tie, and the primary caregiving parent preferences are all meant to enable courts to identify who has been or is most likely to be responsible for the child's care. But only the primary caregiver preference explicitly identifies the evidence essential for assuring that this function will be served. There is no presumption to overcome in order to harmonize a placement decision with its purpose.* Finally, the guidelines and the relatively objective factors to be considered are visible and open to challenge in courts and legislatures.

FAMILY COURTS

Family court judges, whether applying a gender-based preference or a preference for the primary parent, will continue to consider and in some cases require the testimony of experts in child

*The child's need for continuity might go unrecognized and unmet in applying the blood-tie and gender-related presumptive preferences because neither incorporates its function in its formulation. See court's discussion, *Ross v. Hoffman,* p. 58, *supra.*[23]

development.*[24] But as the appellate judge in *Ross v. Hoffman* emphasized, it is always necessary to question the basis of expert testimony. He warned that reliance on the work of psychiatrists, psychologists, and trained social workers "should not be too obsequious or too routine. . . ."†[26]

A similar warning against overreliance on experts may be implicit in one family court judge's observation: "Whenever I ask the Child Guidance Clinic to make an evaluation I know in nine cases out of ten what the report of the Clinic's psychiatric–social worker team will recommend." "That is why," he added, "I seldom send cases to the Clinic for assessment."

This statement could have several different meanings. The judge may mean that he doesn't want to hear what he "knows" the Clinic will report because it almost always conflicts with his personal preference for the outcome of a child placement case. Or he may mean that he does not believe in child

---

*Even experts in child development, recognizing the limits of their knowledge, may not be able to determine which of two psychological parents is primary. In such cases "a judicially supervised drawing of lots between two equally acceptable psychological parents might be the most rational and least offensive [and least disruptive] process for resolving the hard choice."[25]

†This caveat highlights that the social policy that the law is designed to serve is determined not by the experts but by society through law. For example, the legislature might declare a policy that makes the interests of parents or the family, not the child, paramount in the placement process. Or a legislature might enact a statute that gives a priority to a placement that makes the legal status of adoption superior to safeguarding a long-term care relationship that cannot become adoptive.

development theory at all and that he automatically ignores what experts in the field have to say. Or he may mean that he believes that the Clinic's staff base their reports on personal as opposed to professional judgements, or that they are otherwise incompetent. On the other hand, this family court judge may be pleased with the quality of staff work at the Clinic and mean that since the staff treats like case alike, he himself has over time become able to identify like cases in child development terms and is now equipped to decide many of them without hearing expert testimony. Some of these uses of acquired knowledge are improper; others are not. Thus, the meaning of the judge's reluctance to consult the Clinic must be disclosed and left open to review and challenge. Otherwise his own personal, nonprofessional, or outdated views may determine how he uses the "knowledge" he has acquired.

In a limited way, then, the law may come to reflect explicitly in judicial precedent or in statute the "current" state of knowledge from child development. When guided by such judicial or legislative determinations lawyers and judges perform tasks for which they are trained—construing statutes and interpreting precedents in applying them to individual cases. The law, however, does not adjust automatically to new discoveries in the source discipline. Moreover, law, to the extent that it reveals conclusions rather than information about the special knowledge that underlies it, is prone to misapplication. Therefore, the basis for decisions in law—both statute and precedent—must remain highly visible and open to challenge in legislature and in court. Lawyers, judges, and legislators—indeed, all professional persons in the child placement process—must be careful to ask themselves:

"Does the law reflect the current state of knowledge?"

"Would the application of the precedent or statutory provision in this case serve the purpose for which it was fashioned?"

CHILD DEVELOPMENT PROFESSIONALS USING THEIR KNOWLEDGE OF LAW

CHILD PSYCHIATRIST—Jane

Dr. Hague, a child psychiatrist, was engaged by the court-appointed lawyer for 10-year-old Jane to determine the visitation arrangements with her father that would best serve her interests. Her mother, who had custody, opposed all visits. Dr. Hague interviewed the child and her parents and found that she was suffering from a "destructive loyalty conflict." He concluded that Jane would be hurt more from shuttling between "two enemy camps" than from not seeing her father at all for the time being. Nevertheless, in his report to the court he recommended that she visit her father one afternoon each week.

Dr. Hague made this recommendation because he "knew" that the court "never" denied fathers the right to visit unless—as was not the case here—

there was evidence of physical abuse. He explained, "Had I come out against visits altogether, the judge would not only have ordered them anyway, but also would probably have included overnight visits which would have been even more difficult for Jane to tolerate than day-time visits."

By acting counter to his professional opinion, this child psychiatrist negated the basis for his participation in the proceedings. He denied the court information it ought to have had. In accord with his professional findings, Dr. Hague should have told the court that the least harmful alternative for Jane would be no visits, and said why this was so. He might have added that if the court did decide to order visits, they should not be overnight. In that way he could have used his acquired knowledge without increasing the risk of harm to the child and without depriving the court of his expertise.[27]

CLINICAL PSYCHOLOGIST—Peggy

A divorce court judge asked Dr. Burns, a clinical psychologist, to conduct a family study to help him decide who should have custody of six-year-old Peggy. Her father had been a prisoner of war in Vietnam for the past five years, during which time she lived and thrived in the care of her mother. From these facts alone Dr. Burns was able to conclude that it would be best for Peggy to remain with her mother. But she also knew from prior experience with this court that the judge always demanded that there be clinical assessments based on interviews and psychological tests of parent and child. And she knew from a number of prior decisions that custody orders based on such assessments had a better chance of withstanding appellate scrutiny than those that did not. Although she thought that the court was infringing on her professional judgment as well as disserving Peggy's interests by requiring unnecessary tests, she conducted them.

Dr. Burns had no doubt that the possible harm to Peggy from these gratuitous intrusions was less than the harm that would result if the court were to reject her recommendation.* She decided not to risk Peggy's well-being by using the occasion to educate the court about the undesirability of superfluous examinations.† Unlike the decision of Dr. Hague in Jane's case, her action assured—rather than precluded—that the court would consider the information that she was especially qualified to give.

SOCIAL WORKER—Maria Colwell

The *Report of the Committee of Inquiry* following Maria Colwell's murder by her stepfather uncovers some of the hazards facing child development professionals when they act on their knowledge of the law.[30] The Report discloses that at the time her

---

*Of course, had Dr. Burns believed that there was a risk of substantial harm to Peggy from additional tests, conducting them merely to please the trial judge and to assure that the decision not be overturned on appeal would have been an unjustified use of her knowledge acquired from law.[28]

†Dr. Burns' dilemma was like that confronting child care agencies whose policies, though designed to serve the well-being of children, may hurt a particular child if applied inflexibly.[29]

mother and stepfather sought to recover custody of
Maria, the child care agency had evidence that her
trial visits to her parents had been disastrous and
believed that no change in custody should be made.[31]
Yet, the professional staff of the agency decided not
to oppose the parents' attempt to get custody. "Their
reasoning appeared to be that if [the biological
mother] did not succeed on this first occasion she
would probably do so sooner or later and therefore it
was better to accept the position and seek to control
it."[32]

The "better-to-accept" position of the social
workers was based not upon their social work expertise but upon their perception of the legal process.
Their view was not idiosyncratic. "[I]t was generally
believed," the Committee of Inquiry noted, "that
natural parents had the 'right' to have their child
back from care once they had established that they
were fit to receive it and that this thinking influenced
magistrates court."[33] The social workers' acquired
knowledge of law, though well-founded, should not
have been acted upon. By using this knowledge, they
denied the judge an opportunity to consider their professionally informed finding that moving Maria
would be detrimental to her. They arrogated to themselves a decision that belonged to the judge—whether
to accept or reject their opinions. Furthermore, they
sanctioned an outcome which professionally they
knew to be wrong.

If the social workers had been urged by the attorney for the local authority not to waste their or the
court's time by opposing the mother's petition, they

might have recognized that following this advice would be unprofessional. Yet without such outside pressure they compromised their professional selves and thus subverted the hearing before the court.

Except in the event of disastrous consequences, like those in the Maria Colwell case, such use of knowledge about law often goes unnoticed. Therefore, these experts must be especially alert to recognize when they are about to act on their knowledge from law—and not to do so if it would mean depriving the process of the expertise which alone justified their participation. That is true even when their "legal knowledge" is correct and can be applied to the case before them. Before using their acquired knowledge they should ask themselves in each case:

"Will I be depriving the placement process of the expertise which is the basis for my participation?"

"Will I be increasing the risk of harm to the child if I use or act upon my knowledge from another discipline?"

"Have I made the basis of my decision sufficiently visible so that others may question it?"

LAW AND CHILD DEVELOPMENT PROFESSIONALS TOGETHER ASSESSING THEIR USE OF ACQUIRED KNOWLEDGE—DANNY BYSE

Lessons learned from *Maria Colwell*'s case prompted both law and nonlaw trained participants to reexamine a child care agency's decision to withdraw its petition to terminate the parental rights of Danny Byse's mother.

Danny Byse was born in the infirmary of the state prison where his mother, Angela Byse, was serving a two-year sentence. Shortly after birth, Danny was placed in foster care with Donald and Mary Dumont. His father had no interest in him and was willing to surrender his parental rights. Mrs. Byse, on her release from prison, took Danny out of foster care. But she was unable to care for him properly. Within weeks, seriously ill from neglect of his health needs, he was again placed with the Dumonts. He thrived in their care. Once every two months they took him to visit his mother, who had been reimprisoned on another offense. Two years later she was paroled to a half-way house and sought to reestablish her relationship with Danny.

The Child Care Agency responded with a petition to terminate her parental rights in order to give permanency to Danny's relationship with the Dumonts, who wished to adopt him. This decision rested on an assessment by his social worker that Mrs. Byse was unlikely to be able to give Danny the care that his fragile health demanded. The Agency position was reinforced by court-ordered psychiatric evaluations of mother, child, and foster parents. The psychiatrist strongly recommended that Danny and his mother not be reunited. His letter to the court left no doubt that Danny's primary ties were with the Dumonts and that his return to Mrs. Byse would needlessly place him at risk of "undue emotional stress." More importantly, he warned that Danny's life would be jeopardized because Mrs. Byse had shown herself unable to meet his complicated medical needs.

At a pretrial proceeding the judge who was assigned to hear the case said that he would deny the Agency's petition because the mother "deserved a chance" to show what she could do with the child. The Agency, on the advice of the state's attorney who acted as its lawyer, and with the concurrence of the lawyer for the child, withdrew the petition.

Following the Agency's action, the lawyer for Danny, the social worker assigned to his case, the lawyer for the Agency, and the psychiatrist met to discuss the decision to withdraw the termination petition. The psychiatrist explained why he believed that this decision ran counter to Danny's interests. The social worker said that while her professional knowledge led her to concur with the psychiatrist's assessment, she had agreed to the withdrawal because she was persuaded that "there was no chance of winning." She added:

> In any event, even if I had wanted to persist there was no way of getting the Agency lawyer to pursue the matter.

And, indeed, the Agency lawyer said:

> I would have been unwilling to go forward with the petition under these circumstances even if the professional staff had pressed me to proceed.

Finally, Danny's lawyer said:

> Though I was persuaded by the social worker's report and by the psychiatric evaluation that Danny would be harmed if he were ever returned to his mother, I, too, wanted to withdraw the petition, because it was the wrong time strategically. I knew we would lose. On the basis of the expert opinions I knew that there was no parent–child relationship between Danny and his mother and that it would be harmful to try to forge a bond between them. But though these are statutory grounds for termination, the decision is a discretionary matter. I knew the trial judge meant it when he told us at the pretrial hearing that he would throw out the petition.[34] I also knew that I had no chance of winning an appeal under these circumstances.

When a child's well-being is at stake, a lawyer's prediction that the case will be lost, no matter how well informed, is not sufficient to justify abandoning the case.[35] Here the Child Care Agency ought to have instructed the state's attorney to proceed. And the state's attorney should have pursued his client's wishes, even though he "knew" he would not win.* The social workers for the Agency should not have

---

*If the statute had prohibited termination in such cases, the arena for challenge by the social workers would have been the legislature, not the court.

altered their professional behavior in anticipation of the court's decision. They should not have accepted their attorney's view of what would be best for the child. And the lawyer for Danny, informed by experts in child development about his client's needs, ought to have represented him by insisting on going forward.*

Fortunately, the Agency decided to reinstate its petition to terminate and to make visible its reasons for doing so. As a result of this decision, Danny Byse had an opportunity to have his best interests made secure—an opportunity that would otherwise have been foreclosed. And the judge, despite, and even because of, his pretrial position would be confronted with the evidence of the experts. This evidence, even if ignored by the trial judge, would help assure fair review on appeal and ultimately an informed review by the legislature of how well its child placement law was working.

Professional persons who participate in the child placement process must strike a balance between too general and too specific a definition of disciplines. They must acknowledge the existence of borders and, despite the absence of firm guidelines, must differentiate between situations when they can and when they cannot go beyond those borders.[36]

---

*Neither law nor nonlaw professionals ought to withhold information or avoid participation in court proceedings out of fear of being embarrassed in court either by cross-examination or by association with a "lost cause."

Chapter 5

❖

Dual Role—Ambiguity and Ambivalence

In the previous two chapters we examined situations in which professional persons might not have recognized that they were assigned or were assuming roles in the child placement process that they were not especially qualified to perform. In this chapter our focus shifts to situations in which professionals are assigned or assume two potentially incompatible roles in relation to the same child or family. Though qualified for either, they cannot perform both together without the risk of performing one or even both ineffectively. The danger of dual roles is readily perceived when viewed in terms of any professional person who tries to act on behalf of more than one client in relation to the same matter.

    Although dual roles can raise ethical and constitutional questions, we do not address these here.

Rather we address questions of function.* Can, for example, a social worker use home visits for supportive work with a family and at the same time use those visits to investigate allegations of fraud or child abuse for a state welfare agency?[2] Can a mental health therapist who is treating an abusive parent evaluate, from the child's point of view, the desirability of returning that child to that parent? Can a lawyer effectively advocate (not just communicate) a child's custody preference to a court and at the same time advocate what he himself believes, informed by expert advice and guided by case and statutory law, to be in the child's best interests?†

Our clinical experience suggests that professional persons generally cannot effectively perform such dual roles.[5] Potentially conflicting loyalties tend to prevent either assignment from being faithfully discharged. Therefore we believe that the operative presumption for legislature, agency, and court ought

---

*To the extent such dual roles are workable, constitutional and ethical questions still need to be resolved.[1]

†Many of the cases discussed in Chapters 3 and 4 were not simply illustrations of professionals acting outside of their qualifications. It is possible, for example, that the judge in the *Rose* case was trained not only in law but in child development as well. In that event he would have been qualified to be both judge and expert witness—but not in the same case.[3] The social workers in the *Maria Colwell* case might have been trained in law or informed about law through their experience with the family courts, but they could not serve as professional advisers to the court about the child's needs and at the same time decide what portion of their advice or evidence was relevant to the outcome of the case from the legal—as distinguished from the child development—point of view.[4]

to be against the assignment of dual professional roles. And the presumption for professional participants ought to be against accepting or assuming such roles. The cases that follow are illustrations of the functional unworkability of dual role assignments in the child placement process.

CHILD THERAPIST REFUSING TO SERVE AS CONSULTANT TO THE COURT IN A CUSTODY CASE INVOLVING HIS PATIENT—JOHNNY SLOAN

Johnny, age four and a half, whose divorcing parents were involved in an intense court battle for his custody, had been in psychotherapy with Dr. Bernard Steele for several months. Dr. Steele was trying to understand Johnny's fear of falling asleep and to help him overcome it. In the course of the custody hearing, Judge Rachel Thomas learned that Johnny was in psychotherapy with Dr. Steele. She asked him to provide answers to the following questions about the child's relationship to his parents:

"To which parent is Johnny most closely attached?"

"If he is closely attached to both parents, which parent in the short run and which parent in the long run would best be able to serve his interests?"

Dr. Steele refused to carry out Judge Thomas's request. He said that to do so would jeopardize the therapeutic alliance essential to psychotherapy. The effectiveness of therapy, he explained, "rests on Johnny's belief that what he says and does when we are together is just between us and will be used only to help him to try to get over his fear of sleep. Also, if I have to concentrate on the court's questions, I cannot devote my full attention to my therapeutic function."

For Judge Thomas the purist stance of Dr. Steele seemed precious, especially since she suspected that he already had the information she wanted. Dr. Steele insisted that he could not function as Johnny's therapist if he took on an investigative–reportorial role for the court concerning the custody of his patient. No matter whether he made a fresh investigation or used what he had already learned in therapy, his working relationship—the therapeutic alliance—with Johnny would be impaired. Indeed, it would become difficult for Johnny to benefit from treatment even with a different therapist after such a "betrayal." Dr. Steele added that his special relationship with Johnny might unintentionally cause him to be less than objective if he undertook to answer the court's questions. Thus, he would not serve either the court or Johnny well if he attempted to serve both.[6]

Though not entirely convinced by Dr. Steele's objections, Judge Thomas appointed Dr. Cynthia Fare, a child psychiatrist with no prior relationship to Johnny or his family, to do a custody evaluation. In her report, Dr. Fare cited yet another reason why it was good professional practice for Dr. Steele to have refused the court's assignment. The tests and interviews Dr. Fare had conducted revealed a number of details that might become useful in therapy by being clarified and interpreted over an extended time, but which were not otherwise usable. Dr. Fare could easily put these details aside. But Dr. Steele, having already begun to consider these fine points in therapeutic terms, would have found it difficult to disregard them when answering the court's questions. His information overload would have needlessly complicated his custody evaluation. At worst such refinements could divert and confuse; at best they were unnecessary. Deciding the question of custody required findings on which parent was primary and which parent "wanted" the child—not interpretations of Johnny's unconscious that might become useful in treatment but were too unreliable and tentative to be used as placement data.

PSYCHIATRIST AND SOCIAL WORKER ASSUMING DUAL ROLES—KAREN SPENCER

After Karen Spencer had been murdered by her mother, Professor J. D. McClean issued a report to the Derbyshire County Council and Derbyshire Health Authority:[7]

> Karen Spencer was born on 4 December 1975. She had to remain in hospital for some 5 weeks but went home to her parents, Marilyn and David Spencer, on 9 January 1976. On 19 February 1976 she was admitted to hospital with injuries, including a fractured skull, inflicted by her mother. Karen remained in hospital until the end of March and during that time a care order was made, placing her in the care of the

local authority, the Derbyshire County Council. On discharge from hospital Karen was placed with foster parents. She remained with them for twelve months, but was at home with her natural parents for visits most weekends and for longer periods at holiday times. The length of the visits gradually increased until at the end of March 1977 Karen was home on trial on a full-time basis. On 16 April 1977 she was again assaulted by her mother and sustained severe head injuries from which she died three days later.[8]

The Report disclosed that the social worker who was charged with Karen's welfare had also counseled her parents. The social worker and the Consultant Psychiatrist were anxious to give the Spencers "the feeling of progress, something to reward their initiative . . . , something to avert the feeling that 'authority' was not committed to helping them, some incentive for greater efforts in future."[9] The Consultant Psychiatrist, it appears, had also assumed a dual role:

In August and September the Consultant Psychiatrist received requests for a psychiatric assessment from the General Practitioner, the Social Worker, and from the Spencer's Solicitor. The formal position appears to have been that the Psychiatric Report was prepared at the request of the social services department, and it is addressed to the Social Worker. The two

Solicitors were clear that the Consultant Psychiatrist was the department's witness. But not everyone shared that view. The Area Officer annotated one copy of the report: "[The Consultant Psychiatrist] present in court and prepared to give evidence on behalf of mother," and the Consultant Psychiatrist himself was quite clear in his evidence to me that he was acting for Mrs. Spencer. When pressed he said that he was in a sense working with the Social Worker and taking a global view, but that he had been approached by her Solicitor and regarded himself as representing her; but all the professionals involved were friends, "all were trying to do what was best."

Professor McClean continued:

> I have presented in some little detail this interesting difference of emphasis as to the Consultant Psychiatrist's role. I make it quite clear that I am not suggesting any impropriety, or even any real confusion. There is, I believe, always an element of tension, or ambiguity, when a professional (and it can be a lawyer as easily as a medical man or a social worker) owes duties to his client, with whom he will have a continuing relationship, and to the court and other agencies."[10]

We do not agree that there was no "real confusion." Indeed, the hazard of assuming that the Consultant could at the same time adequately represent Karen's needs and those of the parents who had abused her is apparent in his psychiatric report:

> Having regard to Mrs. Spencer's personality and the tendency she has had to act impulsively when under stress, it would seem at first that there has been little time since February for her and her husband to develop a stable relationship which would reassure the Social Services that the child would no longer be at risk. On the other hand my feelings after the interview were that they had responded fairly well to [the Social Worker's] counseling and I am more optimistic about their ability to cope in the future. I would agree that to have the baby home on a permanent basis immediately would be unwise but I think that they need more incentive than they are getting at the moment. In my view I do not think Karen would be at risk if the time she spent with her parents was increased. Mrs. Spencer seems willing and anxious to receive help and guidance and if this were available, I would think her confidence and her general ability in dealing with the day to day problems when looking after a child would develop. I also believe that it is important for the marriage that such an incentive be made available, the resentment which Mr. Spencer still feels would then dissipate more quickly.[11]

Neither the social worker nor the Consultant Psychiatrist should have been responsible for both helping Mrs. Spencer regain custody of Karen and making the determination of whether it was safe for Karen to be returned to her care. The Consultant Psychiatrist should have recognized that he could not act on behalf of everyone who had approached him. The judge should have considered whether the psychiatric assessment of Karen's needs was contaminated by his joining the social worker in "a therapeutic plot" to help Karen's parents.[12] With this confusion about roles unresolved, neither the Spencer parents nor the social services department had reason to trust the Consultant Psychiatrist to do a good job. For the McClean Report to observe that the psychiatrist's "whole report [is] a touch optimistic"[13] understates the problem. In the "plot" and the "optimism" there was compromise in the worst sense. The consultants' obligations were split between making an investigation of Karen's need to be protected from the Spencers and providing the Spencers with help to save their marriage and to regain custody and care of Karen. That duality could not help but influence his interpretation of what he observed and what he reported to the court. As a result of the psychiatrist's dual and divided allegiances, Karen and her parents were ill served.

TWO CANADIAN JUDGES EXAMINE DUAL ROLE OF LAWYER FOR CHILDREN

In *In the Matter of Roy M.C., Jennifer C., Shannon C., and Jason C.*, the judge sought to clarify the role of counsel in child placement cases.[14] Lawyers for the Catholic Children's Aid Society, for the mother of four children, and for the Official Guardian each advocated a different position with regard to the care and custody of the children. With respect to the Official Guardian for the children, Judge Karswick asked:

> [D]oes counsel have an obligation to advocate the child's stated position or does he have the obligation to *also* state his own views of what is in the best interests of the child, discuss the evidence in support of that position and adduce all evidence which bears on the issue of the best interest of the child, even though it may be unfavourable to the child's views, preferences or instructions. . . .

* * *

> When one considers the fundamental importance of this issue of custody for both the family and the community I do not think that the Court can, nor should it, direct the child's counsel to take a strict adversarial role and act as "mouthpiece," blindly advocating a view, preference or instructions which confound or shock his professional opinion of what is in the best interest of the child. It makes eminently good sense to have counsel take an active, real and positive role in the social context of the Family Court, and as Officers of this Court, assume the obligation to adduce all relevant and material evidence on the issue of what is in the best interest of the child, and, when called

upon, to express a professional and responsible view of what that disposition should be.[15]

Judge Karswick apparently did not consider that though a lawyer may be able to *communicate* to a judge both the preference of his child client and his own professionally informed view of the child's "best interests," a lawyer cannot effectively *advocate* both unless they happen to coincide.

In *Re W.*, Judge Abella of the Ontario Provincial Court was specifically asked to clarify the task of the child's legal representative.[16] The child's lawyer had declared that he would support the application of the Children's Aid Society for Crown wardship of a seven-year-old girl. "She also stated that she would be representing the child by presenting not only the child's wishes, but her own perception of the child's best interests as well. It was to this duality of role that mother's counsel [who opposed the wardship application] addressed himself in requesting a clearer delineation of function in order to prepare his own case."[17] Judge Abella, unlike Judge Karswick, concluded that though a child's ambivalence or inability to instruct counsel required "a degree of flexibility in a child's lawyer's role as articulator of his or her client's wishes,"[18] that flexibility did not extend to the lawyer's advocating his own views when they conflicted with those of his child client. The judge observed:

So long as the forum is the courtroom, the child's lawyer should represent his or her young client in a way which reflects equal participation with the other parties in this forum.

Representing a client in these cases usually involves executing a client's instructions and, without being misleading, attempting to show through the evidence that these instructions or wishes best match the child's needs. In other words, a mother who wishes custody of her child expects her lawyer to present her case in such a way that her wishes are shown to be in the best interests of the child. It is, in most cases, an articulation of the client's rather than the lawyer's subjective assessment. It should be no different when the client is a child. Where, therefore, the child has expressed definite views, these views, rather than those of the child's lawyer, should determine what is conveyed to the court. The child's advocate is the legal architect who constructs a case based on the client's views.

In its purest form, that means that the child's lawyer should present and implement a client's instructions to the best of his or her ability. And this, in turn, involves indicating to the court the child's concerns, wishes and opinions. It involves, further, presenting to the court accurate and complete evidence which is consistent with the child's position.[19]

Though we do not share Judge Abella's view of the lawyer's role as advocate of the child's wishes,*

---

*In *Before the Best Interests of the Child,* we argue "that an integral part of the autonomy of parents is their authority and we do share her, rather than Judge Karswick's, position that a lawyer cannot at one and the same time effectively advocate the child's preference and his own professionally informed assessment of "best interests." But in spite of her position she assigns a dual role to counsel for the child when she concludes:

> This case involves a seven-year-old girl who expresses ambivalence about where she wants to live. She has offered no clear instructions to her lawyer. Counsel's role in protecting her client's interests would include, therefore, articulating, exploring and attempting to explain this conflict to the court by evidentiary means [advocacy of the client's wishes]. Then, having heard the evidence of all parties, [counsel] could further assist the court by offering in final sub-

---

presumed capacity to determine whether and how to meet the legal care needs of their child." Under such circumstances, counsel for the child advocates what the parents believe to be in the child's best interests. We further argue that when counsel for the child is imposed without considering parental wishes, as in Judge Karswick's case, "counsel must turn to the court and to the legislature for the guidance he would normally receive from autonomous parents. . . . [He] may look to the parents and the child as sources of information but not for instructions. . . . Children are by definition persons in need of adult caretakers who determine what is best for them. . . . Like an autonomous parent, the court must advise counsel. But it must advise as the child placement statutes direct."[20] Thus the role we would assign to court-imposed counsel for a child is to advocate what, in accord with statutory and case law, is in the child's best interests. But our view of the role of counsel for the child is not the issue here—only whether counsel can assume or be assigned to play two potentially conflicting advocacy roles at the same time for the same child.

missions her assessment of what the evidence reveals to be in her client's "best interests" [advocacy of lawyer's own perception of best interests].[21]

If the child's lawyer advocates that the child has no preference and if the court believes that it needs an "assessment of what the evidence reveals would be in the [child's] 'best' interests,"[22] that task, following Judge Abella's own reasoning, should be assigned to a different lawyer.* Such an arrangement would diminish the risk of the child's lawyer finding "no clear preference" when his client's expressed preference conflicted with his own view of "best interest."

Professional participants must be alert to ask and answer this question:

"Am I [Are you] assuming, assigning, or being assigned more than one role in relation to the same family or child?"

This need to confront and avoid dual assignments reflects one of the differences between the role of the professional person and that of ordinary devoted parents. In every intact family, for example, parents inevitably take some actions that appear to be for the primary benefit of mother, father, or a particular child, even though another child's interest, viewed in isolation, might call for different conduct.

---

*Had Judge Abella adopted the view that counsel for the child was to advocate the child's best interests, rather than to be his "mouthpiece," no duality problem would have arisen.

That is compromise in the best sense—by acting in the interest of family integrity parents serve the overriding interest each of the children has in that family.[23] But in the child placement process, dual role assignments result in compromise in the worst sense, serving no one's best interests. Whenever doubt exists about the incompatibility of two roles, they should be performed by different persons.[24] In the interests of the child, professional participants ought not to be handicapped by being placed—or by placing themselves—in professionally ambiguous positions.

Chapter 6

❊

No License to Act as Parents

Professional participants in the child placement process do not, either individually or collectively, make or make up for a parent. They are specialists, not generalists.* They are neither qualified nor authorized to act with a parent's discretion and prerogatives. Yet they sometimes do. This may be because

*Our view of the parent as the essential generalist in relation to the professional participant in the child placement process is not unlike Wendell Berry's view that the "best farming requires a *farmer*—a husbandman, a nurturer—not a technician or businessman. A technician or a businessman—given the necessary abilities and ambitions—can be made in a little while, by training. A good farmer, on the other hand, is a cultural product; he is made by a sort of training, certainly, in what his time imposes or demands, but he is also made by generations of experience. This essential experience can only be accumulated, tested, preserved, handed down in settled households, friendships, and communities that are deliberately and carefully native to their own ground, in which the past has prepared the present and the present safeguards the future."[1]

good professional work requires humanity as well as expertise and because their assignments often entail performing parentlike tasks that place them in ambiguous relationships with both children and parents.[2] Under such circumstances judges, lawyers, social workers, and child development specialists may unwittingly use their authority to act "the good parent," especially if they find a child (or, indeed, a parent) particularly appealing, annoying, or pathetic. The professionals' challenge, as nonparents, is how to be caring without taking unnecessary control of the life of the child for whom they do not and cannot take full responsibility.[3]

Professional persons may assume the parental prerogatives *directly*, in their contacts with the child, or *indirectly*, by imposing their will on his parents. They may, for example, use their direct contact with a child to discipline him, not as psychologists might because they seek to further therapeutic goals, or as judges might because they must maintain order in the courtroom, but because they consider him "spoiled," "unruly," or "ungrateful." And professionals sometimes use their indirect relationships with children to make parental decisions about family life-style—for example, when trial judges order a joint custody arrangement that neither parent has sought.[4]

When professional persons, in direct contact with a child, must perform parentlike tasks during home or office visits or court proceedings, the child can quickly become confused. Two child development experts were reminded of this problem when they interviewed Jim, age six. Having been asked to tell the court which of Jim's parents was his primary caregiver, they saw Jim in his own room at home. As part of their evaluation, they sat on the floor and enthusiastically joined him in play. As Jim pushed a large toy automobile around the room, one of them asked:

"Where are you going?"

"On a picnic."

"Whom do you want most to go with you?"

"The two of you."

When the professionals' direct contacts with the child are more intense and of longer duration than in a court-ordered evaluation, it is even more difficult to avoid the semblance of the parental role. Therapists in particular face a special problem in their efforts to establish trust with a child patient.[5] A therapist in training said to a five-year-old boy, during a treatment hour, "I love you—I'll always love you even when you're naughty." During daily meetings this therapist let the child hug her and climb on her body. The therapist knew that what she did was for treatment purposes, but the child may not have understood this. He might have felt that she would always be available—like a parent. When this therapist then stopped seeing him not because his treatment was complete* but because she had completed

*Completing treatment would include helping the child understand the limits and limitations of their relationship.

her training, he had good reason to feel betrayed. The result of such betrayal for a child is that his ability to trust may be impaired.*[6]

Parental authority is supervened to some extent when professionals implement, for example, laws that mandate the removal of neglected or abused children, or that favor the rights of natural parents as against long-term foster parents. But no matter how extensive such authorized supervention may be, the problem of gratuitous invasions of parental prerogatives remains.

Judge Dembitz of the New York Family Court recognized the danger of unnecessarily assuming a parental role, albeit an indirect one, in the case of *Melissa M.*[8] She ordered the four-and-a-half-year-old child to be removed from her foster family and to be placed with her natural father and his new wife. Melissa's foster parents then sought a court order allowing them to visit. Melissa's new parents said that visits would disrupt their family life and confuse the child. Though Judge Dembitz found that such

---

*To a lesser degree lawyers representing children over an extended period of time may engender similar confusion in their child clients. This is illustrated by the comments of an Australian judge addressing a conference of child placement professionals. In praising counsel appointed by her to represent a child whose parents were separated, she said:

"[It] came through to me in the process of hearing the case that one of the little girls who is the subject of a custody dispute wants an order whereby she can live somewhere near the instructing solicitor . . . [laughter]."[7]

Such misperceptions by a child of the professional's role must be recognized and minimized.

visits would be beneficial for Melissa, she refrained from substituting her judgment for that of the custodial parents. Unwilling to intrude, even indirectly, on Melissa's relationship with her new parents, Judge Dembitz said that "the parental decision-making prerogative with 'freedom of personal choice in matters of . . . family life' should be maintained . . . unless there is strong reason for interference with it."[9] She recognized that professionals risk injury to parent–child ties if they ignore the meaning of family integrity for a child.[10]

The cases that follow illustrate how some professionals may disregard the fact that though their assigned tasks may be highly significant, their relationships to the children they serve are not permanent commitments. Unlike Judge Dembitz, they sometimes forget that the child is not their own.

TAKING THE PARENTAL PREROGATIVE IN DIRECT CONTACT WITH THE CHILD

JUDGES—EMILY

In a post-divorce visitation dispute Emily, age ten, was interviewed by Family Court Judge Dixon in compliance with the statutory mandate that the preference of older children be taken into account. After the interview Judge Dixon told her parents and their lawyers:

> Emily is a very nice, bright little girl. She has told me what she feels about the visits and I

have explained my decision to her—that visits with her father must continue. *I have also told her that if she has any problems with the visits*—if either her mother or her father make things difficult—*she may come to me at any time and talk to me.* I want both parents to know that I will not allow them to let this little girl suffer from their continued warfare.

Some months later Emily's father went back to court because his daughter refused to see him and her mother would not force her to visit. The mother's lawyer asked Judge Dixon to hear the case because he had already interviewed Emily and was familiar with the circumstances. He refused. He said that he was about to go on an extended vacation and had no time. The lawyer explained that Emily was anxious to talk to him about the visits and reminded him of his promise that she might speak to him at any time. He replied:

Let her talk to Judge Clement, who will be hearing cases while I am away. He is as good a judge as I am.

Judge Dixon misled Emily—she believed that he would be available, as a parent might be, when she needed him. He may have thought he was being understanding and sensitive when he made the promise. He may have felt that implicit in his invitation was the qualification, "if I am not away and if I do not have too many other cases to work on." But Emily had no reason to perceive his "promise" that way. In effect Judge Dixon invited Emily to trust him during a difficult time and then betrayed her.[11] While judges may consider themselves functionally interchangeable with one another, children do not necessarily see them that way.*[12]

The case was then heard by Judge Clement.† He was advised that Emily had been excused from school to talk with him, and that she was waiting in the corridor outside the courtroom, anxious to be heard. He decided, however, to hear her parents first. From them he learned that Emily was adamant in refusing to visit her father, though they disagreed about the reason for this. After several hours of testimony, Judge Clement announced that he would adjourn the hearing until the next day because he now had to hear another case. The lawyer for Emily's mother reminded him that Emily had been waiting for a very long time and asked him to interview her before moving to the other case. Judge Clement replied:

> Let her mother bring her back tomorrow. From what I have learned here today I think it may do Emily some good to make her wait.

---

*Even if the judge had honored his promise, a problem of gratuitous intrusion on Emily's relationship with her parents would remain. By interposing himself between Emily and her parents Judge Dixon might have been undermining their opportunity to work out their own difficulties with the visits he ordered.[13]

†When a child is passed from one judge to another, the new judge should be informed about any representations or promises made by other judges to the child.

He had apparently decided that she was a spoiled child and thought that keeping her waiting outside of his court all day would teach her a lesson. He took a parent's liberties without authority and without a parent's knowledge of Emily. He might have believed that she needed disciplining, but he was not entitled to act on that belief.

When Judge Clement interviewed Emily the following day, he told her:

> You are too young to know what is good for you. You had better visit your father next Sunday; otherwise I will have your mother punished.

Though the judge had authority to order Emily to visit her father, he went beyond his authority and entered her parents' domain when he sought to "educate" her by saying that she was too young to know what was good for her. Further, he intruded on the mother's prerogative by telling Emily the probable consequences of a refusal to obey his order. He did not recognize that Emily must be able to look to her mother as responsible for her, even with regard to court orders. Though parental autonomy is limited by law, it is the province of parents, not of judges, to translate for their children the demands of the law and how these should be met.[14]

Both judges took parental license with Emily—Judge Dixon when he sought to comfort her, and Judge Clement when he attempted to discipline her and to give her insight about herself. Though the intrusiveness of such behavior is clear upon reflection, in practice it may easily go unnoticed by the offending, yet well-meaning, professional person and unchallenged by the intimidated or bewildered parent or child.

FOSTER PARENTS—Rosalie

A child's relationship with foster parents during the placement process is likely to be more intense and more protracted than that with a judge or a lawyer. Foster parents are intended to provide temporary care in a family setting. Their professional assignment may either be to keep alive the foster child's ties to absent parents or to prepare him for permanent placement with an adopting family. Their assignment in both situations requires them to provide full-time, day and night, care for the child in their home. They cannot for long maintain their professional identity; rather they will become "real" parents in their own as well as the child's eyes. Over time, their direct contact with the child may unavoidably obliterate the professional relationship and justify their assertion of parental prerogatives.[15]

Rosalie, a one-year-old child, had been abandoned at birth. Pending adoption, she had been placed by the State's Child and Youth Agency with Mr. and Mrs. Trager who had successfully cared for several children who were waiting to be adopted. The Tragers knew that they were supposed to help Rosalie develop to the best of her ability. They had every intention of cooperating in the adoption plan, as they had many times before. But they "failed." Rosalie needed a great deal of medical attention in the first few months and at one point almost died. In caring for her special needs, the Tragers became devoted to her, as did their own children. An intense and reciprocal feeling of closeness spread through the entire family. Indeed, one of the Trager children wrote the director of the Agency urging that they be allowed to adopt her. Mrs. Trager initially thought that they should stick with their agreement to provide only foster care and that her family was already large enough with three children. But Rosalie "won her over" and she "fell in love with her," as had Mr. Trager and the children.

The Tragers had, necessarily and unavoidably, ceased to be professional parents and had become her real parents. Rosalie was thriving in their care and by this time could in no way have experienced it as temporary. Fortunately for her, the Agency decided not to oppose their petition for adoption.*

TAKING THE PARENTAL PREROGATIVE IN INDIRECT CONTACT WITH THE CHILD

JUDGES—AKI and EDGAR

In a post-divorce custody dispute between a Japanese mother and an American father, the father sought to regain care of their two children, Aki and Edgar. His action was triggered by his ex-wife's plan

*Foster care is intended to be limited to placements that are temporary by a child's sense of time and, as professionals, foster parents must be trained and prepared to give up the child even though they may have grown to love him during that "brief period." When the period of care is no longer temporary from the child's point of view, foster parents become "real" parents for the child and should be so recognized.[16]

to move to another part of the United States. A report to the court by its family relations officer spoke unfavorably of the mother, in large part because she had the children sleep on the floor. Because of this sleeping arrangement, the judge requested a psychiatric evaluation and postponed the hearing. The psychiatric report said that the mother was the primary psychological parent and explained that Aki and Edgar slept on the floor on tatami mats in keeping with Japanese custom.

When the time came for the hearing, another judge presided. He announced that he did not believe in "psychiatric stuff" and refused to look at the report. He told the mother to raise Aki and Edgar as "good Americans" and instructed the father to help her do so by buying proper beds for them. The judge infringed on the parental role by giving unsolicited instructions on how they should raise their children. Even if he believed that it was healthier to sleep in beds than on tatami mats, it was none of his business. His instructions were unrelated to any legitimate goal of the child placement process.[17]

TAKING THE PARENTAL PREROGATIVE IN DIRECT AND INDIRECT CONTACT WITH THE CHILD

CHILD PSYCHIATRISTS AND JUDGES—RANDALL COOPER

A professional person's contact with a child in the placement process may be both direct and indirect. Randall, age seven, whose parents were in bitter dispute over his custody, had a long history of poor behavior. Since his parents' separation a year earlier, he had been in treatment with Dr. Biddle, a child psychiatrist. The court asked Dr. James, also a child psychiatrist, to prepare an evaluation to assist in determining which of his parents should have custody.* Dr. James was sensitive to the risks of intrusion—direct and indirect—on Randall's already troubled relationships with his mother and father as well as on his relationship to Dr. Biddle. In his report to the court, Dr. James said that Randall had been "quickly able to form a relationship" to him during two diagnostic play interviews. He decided against additional interviews "because of Randall's growing attachment and his obvious confusion about my role." From these two play sessions he had learned enough, he said, to know that Randall was clearly attached to both parents, was torn between them, was near panic about the dispute, and needed to remain in treatment.

During the course of his interviews with each parent, Dr. James had recommended to them that Randall remain in therapy. He reported that Mrs. Cooper, who had originally engaged Dr. Biddle, shared his view that treatment continue; and that Mr. Cooper, though he had no objection to treatment, believed that it was unnecessary and did not intend to pay for it. Dr. James said that both Mr. and Mrs. Cooper were loving parents. However, he explained to

*Dr. Biddle had declined to conduct the evaluation. He indicated that his therapeutic work with Randall would be jeopardized if it were not kept separate from the custody dispute.[18]

the court that Randall's interests would be best served by his mother because she understood his need for therapy and because it was more likely to be effective with parental support.

Dr. James closed his report to the court by stating: "It is imperative that Randall remain in treatment." This sentence underlines his recommendation that Mrs. Cooper continue as primary caregiver. He did not suggest that treatment be a condition for custody, but he used her attitude toward treatment as one criterion for selecting the custodial parent. His assertion that Randall needed treatment might, however, have been mistakenly read as a recommendation—something often found in psychiatric evaluations—that the court *order* the custodial parent to provide for therapy.* Such restraints invade a parental prerogative, usurping a decision that ultimately must be left to parents except, of course, in cases of proven neglect or other statutory grounds for intervention. Custody was determined, after all, to provide Randall with a parent responsible for deciding what would be best for him on a day-to-day basis.[20]

Dr. James might have reduced the risk of his report being misread as recommending that the court make therapy a requisite of custody had he added: "Whether and with whom Randall should be in therapy is a decision for the parent who is awarded cus-

---

*Child psychiatrists and other professional persons sometimes fail to distinguish between situations in which parents on their own seek advice—which they are free to accept or reject—and situations in which courts order psychiatric evaluation or treatment.[19]

tody even if—indeed especially if—the court chooses his father."

Professional persons, whether in direct or indirect contact with children in the placement process, must avoid gratuitous assertions of parental prerogatives. The framework of the placement system makes this difficult.* When the child placement process is invoked, parental autonomy is challenged and the parental role is easily disrupted. Professional participants are made responsible by statute and by judicial precedent for ordering and enforcing conditions of custody with regard to matters parents usually determine. Though professional persons may have "to live with their decisions in the sense that they know what they have done, they don't often know what it means to the people in the sense that they don't have to live with the people. . . ."[21] They don't have the opportunity to respond to changing needs in the give-and-take of a day-to-day family relationship and to correct, if they could, their mistakes of judgment. Restraint in the exercise of such parentlike authority is the hallmark of good professional work.[22]

Therefore, professional participants in the child placement process must, in each case, ask themselves and each other:

---

*In other than child placement situations, lawyers, child psychiatrists, and social workers recognize that they cannot effectively treat their child patients or clients as if they were their own children. Indeed, they avoid serving their own children in recognition of the risks that come from obscuring the difference between members of their family and their patients or clients.

"Are we acting to further our professional assignments or are we usurping the parent's prerogative?"

"How can we do our jobs without confusing the child about the extent and meaning of our relationships with him—without harming his relationship to his parents, to his family?"

"Do we mean what we say to the child? Do we intend to keep the promise we made? Even if we do, should we make it?"

By addressing these questions, professional persons can help assure that the degree of intrusion on family integrity will be no greater than that which is necessary to fulfill the function of the state's intervention.[23] Minimizing this intrusion is in the child's best interest.

Chapter 7

❀

Softhearted and Hardheaded

In the last chapter we noted without elaborating that "good professional work requires humanity as well as expertise."[1] Put somewhat differently, the good professional person in the child placement process must be both softhearted and hardheaded. These characteristics complement rather than contradict each other. The professional person whose facile sympathy interferes with his making unpalatable, though necessary, choices is neither hardheaded nor softhearted.[2] The expert who makes hard choices and implements them with kindness and sympathy to the adult or child whom they may hurt is both. The softhearted factor rests on the capacity of professional persons to draw on their emotions in ways which are not exploitative of themselves or of those they serve—to promise or imply no more than they are able and willing to provide. Thus, a judge who comforts a child about to be placed by assuring him that "you can

109

come to see me any time and talk to me" must be prepared, as the judge who made such a promise in Emily's case was not, to carry out his promise.[3]

Softheartedness cannot be mechanized. It requires understanding, genuine humanness, honest sympathy. Humanness is not evidenced by lawyers, doctors, social workers, nurses, and other professional persons who think that they can establish rapport with new adult clients or patients by automatically calling them by their first names. It is not that the use of the first name is always inappropriate. Rather, such policies "generally applied (applied, that is, without consideration of differences) are experienced as indifference."[4] If the softhearted is to complement the hardheaded component of their relationships, professionals must be responsive to the individual needs, circumstances, and characteristics of the persons with whom they deal.[5] This capacity is illustrated by the three cases that follow.

SOFTHEARTEDNESS IN THE WAY A JUDGE ANNOUNCES HIS DECISION—Maggie

Judge Tim Murphy had to decide whether nine-year-old Maggie should remain with her foster parents, with whom she had lived since her eighth day of life, or be returned to her biological mother. Having found, following a four-day hearing, that it would not be in Maggie's interest to be returned to her mother, Judge Murphy asked the parties to come to his chambers. He immediately informed them of his decision. He departed from his usual practice of keeping the parties waiting until he had time to write and file his opinion. He modified this procedure in order to end as quickly as possible the painful uncertainty under which Maggie and her parents, both foster and biological, had been living. Thus he spared them more than a month of long days and nights of anxiously wondering what their fates would be. This softhearted response in no way infringed on the hardheaded choice he had made as judge.[6]

AN INSTITUTION PROMOTES SOFTHEARTEDNESS IN ITS CARE OF CHILDREN

The pediatric unit of the Royal Hobart Hospital in Tasmania, Australia provides an example of how the softhearted factor can become an integral component of a hardheaded institutional setting. The hospital recognized that "child care requires that: (a) children receive rapid, efficient and effective investigation and management of the condition which necessitated their admission [the hardheaded factor]; [and] (b) provision is made for the other needs of children and their families. These needs must cover the intellectual, emotional, and social requirements of children [the softhearted factor]."[7] The hospital recognized that "[m]odern therapy may be highly effective, but it often involves the usage of drugs and equipment which in themselves may produce stress to young patients and their relatives."[8]

To assure that the *individual needs of different*

children are met, parents are asked to complete a personal information sheet containing such details as the child's food likes and dislikes, sleeping times and position, favorite toys and games, words for wanting to go to the toilet, perception of his illness and preferred ways of being comforted when in distress.[9] Further, sensitive to the fears of *all children:*

> [In order to] make the atmosphere less threatening . . . doctors and medical students do not wear white coats and nurses wear attractive aprons over their uniforms. Children are no longer tied into bed, and foldup beds have been purchased so that parents can sleep beside their children. The windows in single cubicles have been curtained and . . . have been turned into parent–child units. . . . We encourage one of the parents to stay with the child and, if space allows it, we take in both if that is what they want. We allow visiting at any time but we recommend suitable rest periods for the patients depending on their ages. Visitors can be siblings, school friends, or any relative, and staff is encouraged to make them feel welcome."[10]

A PHYSICIAN'S SOFTHEARTEDNESS TOWARD A CHILD IN SURGERY—LARRY

Young Dr. Amos Eztin intuitively brought softheartedness to his relationship with four-and-a-half-year-old Larry. Larry was hospitalized for anemia and weight loss. After examination and evaluation he was taken to surgery for removal of a malignant growth in his stomach. There had been no explicit preparations for the hospitalization, anesthesia, or surgery. It was assumed he was too young to understand.

Larry cried as he was placed on the gurney, and asked Dr. Eztin to stay with him. The young physician had become quite fond of this reflective, charming child and his parents. He accompanied Larry to the operating room where Larry asked at each point what was going to happen next. Dr. Eztin answered as best he could. As the anesthetist prepared to induce Larry, the child was panic stricken. Looking at the masked men and women around him, glancing at those sitting on the benches of the old-fashioned amphitheater, he cried out, "What are you going to do to me?" Dr. Eztin became anxious and self-conscious, but his concern for Larry enabled him to take the child's hand and haltingly explain that the doctors and nurses wanted to help him with the growth in his tummy that made him feel weak and sick. Larry interrupted, crying, "No! Why does the man want me to blow away the funny stuff?" Dr. Eztin explained, "He wants to give you a smell medicine so you can sleep. Then it won't hurt while the doctor takes out the growth in your tummy." Larry cried, "I want Mommy to sing me to sleep!" Dr. Eztin explained, "Mommy can't be here." Larry sobbed, "You sing to me." The young doctor gulped and began to hum Brahms' "Lullaby." Larry quieted down, clutched his doctor's hand, and gradually accepted the anesthesia.

At a time of overwhelming fear, Larry was holding on to his yearning for and memory of a soothing, safe closeness to his mother. He made a desperate effort to use the past as he faced a frightening, dangerous present. Dr. Eztin responded to the child's need for the parent who could not be present.* Realizing that he had not been prepared for this challenge by his academic and clinical education, Dr. Eztin dipped into his own past for those memories, those experiences that would answer Larry's need. Dr. Eztin later reflected, "Isn't it ironic that my mother is the one who prepared me for that situation."

A CHILD CARE WORKER'S SOFTHEARTEDNESS TOWARD A CHILD IN A RESIDENTIAL NURSERY—Tony

Tony's mother had died when he was three, following a long illness which had left her unable to care for him. Before coming to a residential nursery Tony had passed through many foster homes. He had received one shock of separation after another and had finally withdrawn completely into himself. However, he gradually emerged from his shell and became fiercely attached to Mary, one of the nurses who looked after him. His soldier father visited him only rarely. On one such visit, when Tony was almost four years old, his father introduced a young woman to Tony as "your new mummy." When the visit was over, Tony, who was "greatly impressed by his father calling him

---

*Hardheaded policies, like softhearted ones, should be open to question. A review of this hospital policy might consider whether parents should be permitted to accompany their child into the operating room.

'son'," asked: "Mary, will you call me 'son' like my daddy does?" When she said that she would rather not, because he was really not her son, he agreed that she might continue to call him by his pet name, so long as no one else was called by it.[11]

Mary was able to respond to Tony's need for a special relationship with her, without encouraging him to think of her as his mother.

Professional participants, including the administrators and staff of institutions, must ask:

"Is the routine, procedure, or policy essential to our task or does it unnecessarily restrict a child's relationship with his family?"

"Am I about to say something which will unnecessarily undermine a child's relationship to his parents or other adult caregivers?"

"Are my affectionate and positive feelings for the child interfering with my carrying out my professional work?"

"Am I being a warm, decent, caring human being?"

"Am I using the child as an outlet for my own emotional needs?"

If professional persons ignore the limits of their assignments; if they are guided by personal preferences rather than by professional training and experience; if, out of sentimental feeling for the child, they act as if they were the parent they are not, they are not being softhearted. Unaccompanied by hardheaded willingness to face facts, their actions can only bring disappointment to the child.

If professional persons are alert to the danger

of exceeding their competence and authority, if they understand the need for drawing lines and for making their actions both visible to themselves and open to challenge by others, they demonstrate hardheadedness which translates into softheartedness. They will help to ensure for the child whose interests they serve what he needs most—strong bonds with an autonomous parent.

Part Three

The Compleat Professional

Chapter 8

❈

In the Best Interests of the Child

Good professional practice necessitates weighing, balancing, and resolving conflicting demands, expectations, and pressures. We have described and analyzed some of the quandaries that confront professional participants in the child placement process. Awareness of their existence is the first step in their resolution.

In Chapter 1 we describe the "ordinary devoted parent"; we affirm that, ideally, every child should have such parents in order to maximize his chance for healthy development. At the same time, we recognize that parents sometimes fail massively, and that when they do the state is authorized to intervene. Then the parental task may be broken up and assigned to different professional participants in the child placement process. We characterize the parent as the quintessential generalist from whom professional expertise is not demanded, expected, or desired. We ask

the Parent

the professional person to remember that he is not the parent of the child caught up in the placement process. He is not a generalist but a specialist. At the same time we recognize that empathy and warmth are essential to good professional work with children.

In Chapter 2 we ask the professional person to distinguish between professionally informed belief and personal value preferences so that the dogma of one group is not imposed on another in the name of "science." We recognize that it is difficult to separate personal values and professional knowledge and, in turn, to distinguish these from societal values reflected in law. Therefore, we seek to alert professionals and those who engage them to the danger of allowing their reputations as experts to be used to further their personal, nonprofessionally informed, preferences.

In Chapter 3 we discuss the professional person's responsibility for not exceeding his competence and authority by entering the province of other experts or by failing to acknowledge the limitations of his own special knowledge. We want judges and lawyers not to act as adult psychologists or child development experts, and child development experts not to act as judges. When asked to go beyond their competence, professional persons should be prepared to say, "I don't know" or "I can't answer that question." We ask them not to act on the basis of the personal preferences that they might have as adults and parents. Yet we expect these professional persons to reflect wisdom based on their experience not only as

specialists but as human beings possessed of ordinary knowledge.

In Chapter 4 we point out that experts from different fields can and do learn from the experience of
working together in the child placement process.
Child development knowledge has led to the incor-
poration of the primary caregiver preference and its
functional components into child placement law by
statute and judicial precedent, thus equipping lawyers and judges to a limited extent with special
knowledge from another profession. But we caution
that such knowledge, if used at all, must be used explicitly and visibly so that its validity and applicabil-
ity are open to challenge. And we point out that
experience-based knowledge from another discipline,
even though valid and applicable, should not be used,
if to do so would contravene the dictates of the
expert's own professionally informed judgment or
negate the basis for his participation in the child
placement process. Thus, we fault the social worker or
psychiatrist who fails to present to the judge his professional view about a particular placement because
he has learned from experience that this judge will not
listen to him. And we criticize the judge who fails to
order a psychiatric evaluation because he does not
want to hear what he knows the evaluation will find
since it conflicts with his prejudgment of the case. A
workable child placement process will provide for a
conscious, restrained, open, and reviewable use by
professional participants of knowledge acquired from
a discipline not their own.

In Chapter 5 we ask the professional person to be aware of yet another limitation—that he may not be able to perform two different roles in relation to the same family, though each of the roles may be within his professional competence. Thus a social worker is unable effectively to use home visits with a family both for supportive work and for investigating and reporting evidence of child abuse or misrepresentation in obtaining welfare benefits. A lawyer for a child cannot advocate both the child's wishes and his own perception as a lawyer (with the advice of experts in child development and on the basis of statutory and case law) of the child's best interests.

In Chapter 6 we ask the professional person to recognize the difference between the caring expert and the usurper of parental autonomy. We know that he may be assigned parentlike tasks. We ask him to perform these without taking the parent's full prerogatives. In direct contact with the child the professional should behave with warmth and understanding without undermining parental authority and without encouraging the child to form too great an attachment; he must resist the temptation to instruct the child in what he "knows" to be moral, wise, or good behavior lest by doing so he weaken the child's confidence in his parents. We ask the professional person who has indirect contact with the child to avoid unwarranted intrusions in the family. Though parental autonomy may be limited by law, it is the province of parents to translate for their children the demands of the law and whether and how they should be met.

In Chapter 7 we stress that good professional

practice requires humanity as well as expertise—soft-heartedness as well as hardheadedness. The professional person should not be swayed by sympathy, but he must be sympathetic.

These, then, are the apparent contradictions we describe in their multiple guises and situations: The nonparent participant ought not to be swayed from professional standards by personal preference or sympathy for a particular adult or child. He should not stray beyond the boundaries of his own professional training into the territory of another discipline. He should not be guided by his knowledge from another discipline if to do so would be against his own professional judgment. He should not confuse the child he serves by acting like the parent he is not. At the same time, the good professional is expected to bring to his work in the child placement process the wisdom he has acquired through his experience working with families and with other professionals and as a human being, child, adult, and even perhaps as parent. For good work with adults and especially with children, he must be sympathetic, warm, and understanding.

It is in the best interests of the child for all of the professional participants to recognize that neither separately nor together do they make or make up for a parent—even an ordinary, imperfect one. Their special knowledge is general to all children, and their function in the placement process is to enhance each child's opportunity to have a parent whose knowledge is general but to whom the child is special.

Part Four

Appendices

Appendix 1

Carrie Buck's Daughter

By Stephen Jay Gould

*A popular, quasi-scientific idea can be a powerful
tool for injustice.*

The Lord really put it on the line in his preface to that
prototype of all prescription, the Ten Command-
ments:

> ... for I, the Lord thy God, am a jealous God,
> visiting the iniquity of the fathers upon the
> children unto the third and fourth generation of
> them that hate me [Exod. 20:5].

The terror of this statement lies in its patent
unfairness—its promise to punish guiltless offspring
for the misdeeds of their distant forbears.

A different form of guilt by genealogical association attempts to remove this stigma of injustice by

denying a cherished premise of Western thought—
human free will. If offspring are tainted not simply by
the deeds of their parents but by a material form of
evil transferred directly by biological inheritance,
then "the iniquity of the fathers" becomes a signal or
warning for probable misbehavior of their sons. Thus
Plato, while denying that children should suffer
directly for the crimes of their parents, nonetheless
defended the banishment of a man whose father,
grandfather, and great-grandfather had all been con-
demned to death.

It is, perhaps, merely coincidental that both Je-
hovah and Plato chose three generations as their criterion for establishing different forms of guilt by
association. Yet we have a strong folk, or vernacular,
tradition for viewing triple occurrences as minimal
evidence of regularity. We are told that bad things
come in threes. Two may be an accidental association;
three is a pattern. Perhaps, then, we should not won-
der that our own century's most famous pronounce-
ment of blood guilt employed the same criterion—
Oliver Wendell Holmes's defense of compulsory
sterilization in Virginia (Supreme Court decision of
1927 in *Buck v. Bell*): "three generations of imbeciles
are enough."

Restrictions upon immigration, with national
quotas set to discriminate against those deemed mentally unfit by early versions of IQ testing, marked the
greatest triumph of the American eugenics movement—the flawed hereditarian doctrine, so popular
earlier in our century and by no means extinct today
(see my column on Singapore's "great marriage de-

bate," May 1984), that attempted to "improve" our human stock by preventing the propagation of those deemed biologically unfit and encouraging procreation among the supposedly worthy. But the movement to enact and enforce laws for compulsory "eugenic" sterilization had an impact and success scarcely less pronounced. If we could debar the shiftless and the stupid from our shores, we might also prevent the propagation of those similarly afflicted but already here.

The movement for compulsory sterilization began in earnest during the 1890's, abetted by two major factors—the rise of eugenics as an influential political movement and the perfection of safe and simple operations (vasectomy for men and saplingectomy, the cutting and tying of Fallopian tubes, for women) to replace castration and other obvious mutilation. Indiana passed the first sterilization act based on eugenic principles in 1907 (a few states had previously mandated castration as a punitive measure for certain sexual crimes, although such laws were rarely enforced and usually overturned by judicial review). Like so many others to follow, it provided for sterilization of afflicted people residing in the state's "care," either as inmates of mental hospitals and homes for the feebleminded or as inhabitants of prisons. Sterilization could be imposed upon those judged insane, idiotic, imbecilic, or moronic, and upon convicted rapists or criminals when recommended by a board of experts.

By the 1930's, more than thirty states had passed similar laws, often with an expanded list of so-called hereditary defects, including alcoholism and drug addiction in some states, and even blindness and deafness in others. It must be said that these laws were continually challenged and rarely enforced in most states; only California and Virginia applied them zealously. By January 1935, some 20,000 forced "eugenic" sterilizations had been performed in the United States, nearly half in California.

No organization crusaded more vociferously and successfully for these laws than the Eugenics Record Office, the semiofficial arm and repository of data for the eugenics movement in America. Harry Laughlin, superintendent of the Eugenics Record Office, dedicated most of his career to a tireless campaign of writing and lobbying for eugenic sterilization. He hoped, thereby, to eliminate in two generations the genes of what he called the submerged tenth—"the most worthless one-tenth of our present population." He proposed a "model sterilization law" in 1922, designed

> to prevent the procreation of persons socially inadequate from defective inheritance, by authorizing and providing for eugenical sterilization of certain potential parents carrying degenerate hereditary qualities.

This model bill became the prototype for most laws passed in America, although few states cast their net as widely as Laughlin advised. (Laughlin's categories encompassed "blind, including those with seriously impaired vision; deaf, including those with seriously impaired hearing; and dependent, including orphans, ne'er-do-wells, the homeless, tramps, and paupers.") Laughlin's suggestions were better heeded in Nazi Germany, where his model act served as a basis for the infamous and stringently enforced *Erbgesund-heitsrecht,* leading by the eve of World War II to the sterilization of some 375,000 people, most for "congenital feeblemindedness," but including nearly 4,000 for blindness and deafness.

The campaign for forced eugenic sterilization in America reached its climax and height of respectability in 1927, when the Supreme Court, by an 8–1 vote, upheld the Virginia sterilization bill in the case of *Buck v. Bell.* Oliver Wendell Holmes, then in his mid-eighties and the most celebrated jurist in America, wrote the majority opinion with his customary verve and power of style. It included the notorious paragraph, with its chilling tag line, cited ever since as the quintessential statement of eugenic principles. Remembering with pride his own distant experiences as an infantryman in the Civil War, Holmes wrote:

> We have seen more than once that the public welfare may call upon the best citizens for their lives. It would be strange if it could not call upon those who already sap the strength of the state for these lesser sacrifices. . . . It is better for all the world, if instead of waiting to execute degenerate offspring for crime, or to let them starve for their imbecility, society can prevent those who are manifestly unfit from continuing their kind. The principle that sustains com-

pulsory vaccination is broad enough to cover cutting the Fallopian tubes. Three generations of imbeciles are enough.

Who, then, were the famous "three generations of imbeciles," and why should they still compel our interest?

When the state of Virginia passed its compulsory sterilization law in 1924, Carrie Buck, an eighteen-year-old white woman, was an involuntary resident at the State Colony for Epileptics and Feebleminded. As the first person selected for sterilization under the new act, Carrie Buck became the focus for a constitutional challenge launched, in part, by conservative Virginia Christians who held, according to eugenical "modernists," antiquated views about individual preferences and "benevolent" state power. (Simplistic political labels do not apply in this case, and rarely do in general. We usually regard eugenics as a conservative movement and its most vocal critics as members of the left. This alignment has generally held in our own decade. But eugenics, touted in its day as the latest in scientific modernism, attracted many liberals and numbered among its most vociferous critics groups often labeled as reactionary and antiscientific. If any political lesson emerges from these shifting allegiances, we might consider the true inalienability of certain human rights.)

But why was Carrie Buck in the State Colony and why was she selected? Oliver Wendell Holmes

upheld her choice as judicious in the opening lines of
his 1927 opinion:

> Carrie Buck is a feeble-minded white woman
> who was committed to the State Colony. . . .
> She is the daughter of a feeble-minded mother
> in the same institution, and the mother of an il-
> legitimate feeble-minded child.

In short, inheritance stood as the crucial issue
(indeed as the driving force behind all eugenics). For if
measured mental deficiency arose from malnourishment, either of body or mind, and not from tainted
genes, then how could sterilization be justified? If decent food, upbringing, medical care, and education
might make a worthy citizen of Carrie Buck's daughter, how could the State of Virginia justify the sever-
ing of Carrie's Fallopian tubes against her will? (Some
forms of mental deficiency are passed by inheritance
in family lines, but most are not—a scarcely surpris-
ing conclusion when we consider the thousand shocks
that beset fragile humans during their lives, from difficulties in embryonic growth to traumas of birth,
malnourishment, rejection, and poverty. In any case,
no fair-minded person today would credit Laughlin's
social criteria for the identification of hereditary deficiency—ne'er-do-wells, the homeless, tramps, and
paupers—although we shall soon see that Carrie Buck
was committed on these grounds.)

When Carrie Buck's case emerged as the crucial
test of Virginia's law, the chief honchos of eugenics

knew that the time had come to put up or shut up on the crucial issue of inheritance. Thus, the Eugenics Record Office sent Arthur H. Estabrook, their crack fieldworker, to Virginia for a "scientific" study of the case. Harry Laughlin himself provided a deposition, and his brief for inheritance was presented at the local trial that affirmed Virginia's law and later worked its way to the Supreme Court as *Buck v. Bell.*

Laughlin made two major points to the court. First, that Carrie Buck and her mother, Emma Buck, were feebleminded by the Stanford–Binet test of IQ, then in its own infancy. Carrie scored a mental age of nine years, Emma of seven years and eleven months. (These figures ranked them technically as "imbeciles" by definitions of the day, hence Holmes's later choice of words. Imbeciles displayed a mental age of six to nine years; idiots performed worse, morons better, to round out the old nomenclature of mental deficiency.) Second, that most feeblemindedness is inherited, and Carrie Buck surely belonged with this majority. Laughlin reported:

> Generally feeble-mindedness is caused by the inheritance of degenerate qualities; but sometimes it might be caused by environmental factors which are not hereditary. In the case given, the evidence points strongly toward the feeblemindedness and moral delinquency of Carrie Buck being due, primarily, to inheritance and not to environment.

Carrie Buck's daughter was then, and has always been, the pivotal figure of this painful case. As I stated before, we tend (often at our peril) to regard two as potential accident and three as an established pattern. The supposed imbecility of Emma and Carrie might have been coincidental, but the diagnosis of similar deficiency for Vivian Buck (made by a social worker, as we shall see, when Vivian was but six months old) tipped the balance in Laughlin's favor and led Holmes to declare the Buck lineage inherently corrupt by deficient heredity. Vivian sealed the pattern—*three* generations of imbeciles are enough. Besides, had Carrie not given illegitimate birth to Vivian, the issue (in both senses) would never have emerged.

Oliver Wendell Holmes viewed his work with pride. The man so renowned for his principle of judicial restraint, who had proclaimed that freedom must not be curtailed without "clear and present danger"—without the equivalent of falsely yelling "fire" in a crowded theater—wrote of his judgment in *Buck v. Bell:* "I felt that I was getting near the first principle of real reform."

And so the case of *Buck v. Bell* remained for fifty years, a footnote to a moment of American history perhaps best forgotten. And then, in 1980, it reemerged to prick our collective conscience, when Dr. K. Ray Nelson, then director of the Lynchburg Hospital where Carrie Buck was sterilized, researched the records of his institution and discovered that more than 4,000 sterilizations had been performed, the last as late as 1972. He also found Carrie Buck alive, and well near Charlottesville, and her sister Doris, covertly sterilized under the same law (she was told that her operation was for appendicitis), and now, with fierce dignity, dejected and bitter because she had wanted a child more than anything else in her life and had finally, in her old age, learned why she had never conceived.

As scholars and reporters visited Carrie Buck and her sister, what a few experts had known all along became abundantly clear to everyone. Carrie Buck was a woman of obviously normal intelligence. For example, Paul A. Lombardo of the School of Law at the University of Virginia, and a leading scholar of the *Buck v. Bell* case, wrote in a letter to me:

> As for Carrie, when I met her she was reading newspapers daily and joining a more literate friend to assist at regular bouts with the crossword puzzles. She was not a sophisticated woman, and lacked social graces, but mental health professionals who examined her in later life confirmed my impressions that she was neither mentally ill nor retarded.

On what evidence, then, was Carrie Buck consigned to the State Colony for Epileptics and Feeble-Minded on January 23, 1924? I have seen the text of her commitment hearing; it is, to say the least, cursory and contradictory. Beyond the simple and undocumented say-so of her grandparents, and her own brief appearance before a commission of two doctors and a justice of the peace, no evidence was presented. Even the crude and early Stanford-Binet test, so fatally flawed as a measure of innate worth (see my book

The Measure of Man, although the evidence of Carrie's own case suffices) but at least clothed with the aura of quantitative respectability, had not yet been applied.

When we understand why Carrie Buck was committed in January 1924, we can finally comprehend the hidden meaning of her case and its message for us today. The silent key, again and as always, is her daughter Vivian, born on March 28, 1924, and then but an evident bump on her belly. Carrie Buck was one of several illegitimate children borne by her mother, Emma. She grew up with foster parents, J. T. and Alice Dobbs, and continued to live with them, helping out with chores around the house. She was apparently raped by a relative of her foster parents, then blamed for her resultant pregnancy. Almost surely, she was (as they used to say) committed to hide her shame (and her rapist's identity), not because enlightened science had just discovered her true mental status. In short, she was sent away to have her baby. Her case never was about mental deficiency; it was always a matter of sexual morality and social deviance. The annals of her trial and hearing reek with the contempt of the well-off and well-bred for poor people of "loose morals." Who really cared whether Vivian was a baby of normal intelligence; she was the illegitimate child of an illegitimate woman. Two generations of bastards are enough. Harry Laughlin began his "family history" of the Bucks by writing: "These people belong to the shiftless, ignorant and worthless class of anti-social whites of the South."

We know little of Emma Buck and her life, but

we have no more reason to suspect her than her daughter Carrie of true mental deficiency. Their deviance was social and sexual; the charge of imbecility was a cover-up, Mr. Justice Holmes notwithstanding.

We come then to the crux of the case, Carrie's daughter Vivian. What evidence was ever adduced for her mental deficiency? This and only this: At the original trial in late 1924, when Vivian Buck was seven months old, a Miss Wilhelm, social worker for the Red Cross, appeared before the court. She began by stating honestly the true reason for Carrie Buck's commitment:

> Mr. Dobbs, who had charge of the girl, had taken her when a small child, had reported to Miss Duke [the temporary secretary of Public Welfare for Albemarle County] that the girl was pregnant and that he wanted to have her committed somewhere—to have her sent to some institution.

Miss Wilhelm then rendered her judgment of Vivian Buck by comparing her with the normal granddaughter of Mrs. Dobbs, born just three days earlier:

> It is difficult to judge probabilities of a child as young as that, but it seems to me not quite a normal baby. In its appearance—I should say that perhaps my knowledge of the mother may prejudice me in that regard, but I saw the child at the same time as Mrs. Dobbs' daughter's baby, which is only three days older than this

one, and there is a very decided difference in the development of the babies. That was about two weeks ago. There is a look about it that is not quite normal, but just what it is, I can't tell.

This short testimony, and nothing else, formed all the evidence for the crucial third generation of imbeciles. Cross-examination revealed that neither Vivian nor the Dobbs grandchild could walk or talk, and that "Mrs. Dobbs' daughter's baby is a very responsive baby. When you play with it or try to attract its attention—it is a baby that you can play with. The other baby is not. It seems very apathetic and not responsive." Miss Wilhelm then urged Carrie Buck's sterilization: "I think," she said, "it would at least prevent the propagation of her kind." Several years later, Miss Wilhelm denied that she had ever examined Vivian or deemed the child feebleminded.

Unfortunately, Vivian died at age eight of "enteric colitis" (as recorded on her death certificate), an ambiguous diagnosis that could mean many things but may well indicate that she fell victim to one of the preventable childhood diseases of poverty (a grim reminder of the real subject in *Buck v. Bell*). She is therefore mute as a witness in our reassessment of her famous case.

When *Buck v. Bell* resurfaced in 1980, it immediately struck me that Vivian's case was crucial and that evidence for the mental status of a child who died at age eight might best be found in report cards. I have therefore been trying to track down Vivian Buck's school records for the past four years and have finally succeeded. (They were supplied to me by Dr. Paul A. Lombardo, who also sent other documents, including Miss Wilhelm's testimony, and spent several hours answering my questions by mail and Lord knows how much time playing successful detective in re Vivian's school records. I have never met Dr. Lombardo; he did all this work for kindness, collegiality, and love of the game of knowledge, not for expected reward or even requested acknowledgment. In a profession—academics—so often marked by pettiness and silly squabbling over meaningless priorities, this generosity must be recorded and celebrated as a sign of how things can and should be.)

Vivian Buck was adopted by the Dobbs family, who had raised (but later sent away) her mother, Carrie. As Vivian Alice Elaine Dobbs, she attended the Venable Public Elementary School of Charlottesville for four terms, from September 1930 until May 1932, a month before her death. She was a perfectly normal, quite average student, neither particularly outstanding nor much troubled. In those days before grade inflation, when C meant "good, 81–87" (as defined on her report card) rather than barely scraping by, Vivian Dobbs received A's and B's for deportment and C's for all academic subjects but mathematics (which was always difficult for her, and where she scored D) during her first term in Grade 1A, from September 1930 to January 1931. She improved during her second term in 1B, meriting an A in deportment, C in mathematics, and B in all other academic subjects; she was on the honor roll in April 1931. Promoted to 2A, she had trouble during the fall term of 1931, failing mathematics and spelling but receiving A in deportment, B in reading, and C in writing and English. She was "retained in 2A" for the next term—or "left back" as we used to say, and scarcely a sign of imbecility as I remember all my buddies who suffered a similar fate. In any case, she again did well in her final term, with B in deportment, reading, and spelling, and C in writing, English, and mathematics during her last month in school. This offspring of "lewd and immoral" women excelled in deportment and performed adequately, although not brilliantly, in her academic subjects.

In short, we can only agree with the conclusion that Dr. Lombardo has reached in his research on *Buck v. Bell*—there were no imbeciles, not a one, among the three generations of Bucks. I don't know that such correction of cruel but forgotten errors of history counts for much, but it is at least satisfying to learn that forced eugenic sterilization, a procedure of such dubious morality, earned its official justification (and won its most quoted line of rhetoric) on a patent falsehood.

Carrie Buck died last year. By a quirk of fate, and not by memory or design, she was buried just a few steps from her only daughter's grave. In the umpteenth and ultimate verse of a favorite old ballad, a rose and a brier—the sweet and the bitter—emerge from the tombs of Barbara Allen and her lover, twining about each other in the union of death. May Carrie and Vivian, victims in different ways and in the flower of youth, rest together in peace.

Appendix 2

The Autobiography of Malcolm X

By Malcolm X, with Alex Haley

When the state Welfare people began coming to our house, we would come from school sometimes and find them talking with our mother, asking a thousand questions. They acted and looked at her, and at us, and around in our house, in a way that had about it the feeling—at least for me—that we were not people. In their eyesight we were just *things*, that was all.

* * *

. . . She would talk back sharply to the state Welfare people, telling them that she was a grown woman, able to raise her children, that it wasn't necessary for them to keep coming around so much, meddling in our lives. And they didn't like that.

But the monthly Welfare check was their pass. They acted as if they owned us, as if we were their private property. As much as my mother would have liked to, she couldn't keep them out. She would get particularly incensed when they began insisting upon drawing us older children aside, one at a time, out on the porch or somewhere, and asking us questions, or telling us things—against our mother and against each other.

We couldn't understand why, if the state was willing to give us packages of meat, sacks of potatoes and fruit, and cans of all kinds of things, our mother obviously hated to accept. We really couldn't understand. What I later understood was that my mother was making a desperate effort to preserve her pride—and ours.

* * *

About this time, my mother began to be visited by some Seventh Day Adventists who had moved into a house not too far down the road from us.

. . . Like us, they were against eating rabbit and pork; they followed the Mosaic dietary laws. They ate nothing of the flesh without a split hoof, or that didn't chew a cud. We began to go with my mother to the Adventist meetings that were held further out in the country. For us children, I know that the major attraction was the good food they served. But we listened, too.

* * *

Meanwhile, the state Welfare people kept after my mother. By now, she didn't make it any secret that she hated them, and didn't want them in her house. But they exerted their right to come, and I have many, many times reflected upon how, talking to us children, they began to plant the seeds of division in our minds. They would ask such things as who was smarter than the other. And they would ask me why I was "so different."

I think they felt that getting children into foster homes was a legitimate part of their function, and the result would be less troublesome, however they went about it.

And when my mother fought them, they went after her—first, through me. I was their first target. I stole; that implied that I wasn't being taken care of by my mother.

*   *   *

I'm not sure just how or when the idea was first dropped by the Welfare workers that our mother was losing her mind.

But I can distinctly remember hearing "crazy" applied to her by them when they learned that the Negro farmer who was in the next house down the road from us had offered to give us some butchered pork—a whole pig, maybe even two of them—and she had refused. We all heard them call my mother "crazy" to her face for refusing good meat. It meant nothing to them even when she explained that we had never eaten pork, that it was against her religion as a Seventh Day Adventist.

They were as vicious as vultures. They had no

feelings, understanding, compassion, or respect for my mother. They told us, "She's crazy for refusing food." Right then was when our home, our unity, began to disintegrate. We were having a hard time, and I wasn't helping. But we could have made it, we could have stayed together. As bad as I was, as much trouble and worry as I caused my mother, I loved her.

The state people, we found out, had interviewed the Gohannas family, and the Gohannas' had said that they would take me into their home. My mother threw a fit, though, when she heard that—and the home wreckers took cover for a while.

*　*　*

When finally I was sent to the Gohannas' home, at least in a surface way I was glad. I remember that when I left home with the state man, my mother said one thing: "Don't let them feed him any pig."

*　*　*

Soon the state people were making plans to take over all my mother's children. She talked to herself nearly all of the time now, and there was a crowd of new white people entering the picture— always asking questions. They would even visit me at the Gohannas'. They would ask me questions out on the porch, or sitting out in their cars.

Eventually my mother suffered a complete breakdown, and the court orders were finally signed. They took her to the State Mental Hospital at Kalamazoo.

It was seventy-some miles from Lansing, about an hour and a half on the bus. A Judge McClellan in Lansing had authority over me and all of my brothers and sisters. We were "state children," court wards; he had the full say-so over us. A white man in charge of a black man's children! Nothing but legal, modern slavery—however kindly intentioned.

* * *

I truly believe that if ever a state social agency destroyed a family, it destroyed ours. We wanted and tried to stay together. Our home didn't have to be destroyed. But the Welfare, the courts, and their doctor, gave us the one–two–three punch. And ours was not the only case of this kind.

Notes

CHAPTER 1: THE PROBLEM AND OUR QUESTIONS

1. The phrase "ordinary devoted parents" is from D. W. Winnicott, *The Ordinary Devoted Mother and Her Baby* (London: Tavistock Publications, 1949). See J. Goldstein, A. Freud, and A. J. Solnit, *Beyond the Best Interests of the Child* (New York: Free Press, New Edition 1979, p. 7) (hereinafter cited as *Beyond the Best Interests of the Child*) and J. Goldstein, A. Freud, and A. J. Solnit, *Before the Best Interests of the Child* (New York: Free Press, 1979, p. 4) (hereinafter cited as *Before the Best Interests of the Child*).

2. James and Joyce Robertson, *Baby in the Family* (London: Penguin Books, 1982, p. 122) (paragraphing omitted).

    Tillie Olson has described these parental feelings in her story "I Stand Here Ironing," reprinted in *Motherlove,* ed. S. Spinner (Laurel, 1978, p. 216):

    > She was a beautiful baby. She blew shining bubbles of sound. She loved motion, loved light, loved color and music and textures. She would lie on the floor in her blue overalls patting the surface so hard in ecstasy her hands and feet would blur. She was a miracle to me, but when she was eight months old I had to leave her day-

147

times with the woman downstairs to whom she
was no miracle at all. . . .

An anecdote provides a picture of the parental
task not unlike that perceived by the woman downstairs. Early in the Second World War, a young refugee
woman was employed as a mother's helper in an English household. After several weeks she plaintively described her job:

> At 7 o'clock in the morning I have to wake
> the older children. Then I have to help them to
> get dressed. As soon as I've done that, I have to
> run down the stairs to cook breakfast. Hardly
> have I finished with that, I have to run up the
> stairs to bathe and dress the baby. As soon as
> I've done that I have to run down the stairs to
> serve the breakfast. Then I'm expected to wash
> the dishes. No sooner have I finished with that,
> it's time to walk the older children to school.
> Hardly have I returned to the house than it's
> time to run up the stairs and feed the baby and
> make the beds. As soon as I've finished with that
> I have to run down the stairs and cook the lunch,
> serve the lunch, wash the dishes, walk the baby,
> prepare high tea, fetch the children from school,
> serve the tea, wash the dishes—and so it goes on
> all day; up the stairs, down the stairs, in the
> house, outside the house, cleaning, cooking,
> serving meals, feeding children, dressing chil-
> dren, playing with the baby, reading bed-time
> stories—until I go to bed exhausted. And the
> next day it starts all over.

Though parents have similar thoughts at times,
their love for their children usually lightens the burden.

3. See *Before the Best Interests of the Child* (pp. 12-13, 15-25).

4. *Beyond the Best Interests of the Child* (p. 5).

5. *Beyond the Best Interests of the Child* (pp. 53-64).

6. *Beyond the Best Interests of the Child* (pp. 49-52).

7. *Before the Best Interests of the Child* (p. 3).

CHAPTER 2: UNTANGLING PROFESSIONAL AND PERSONAL BELIEFS

1. See Dorothy Burlingham, Preface, *Beyond the Best Interests of the Child* (p. x).

2. *Before the Best Interests of the Child* (pp. 4-5) and see *Beyond the Best Interests of the Child* (pp. 7-8).

   In *Beyond the Best Interests of the Child* (p. 109), our imaginary Judge Baltimore was faced with a conflict between professional knowledge and personal values. In an opinion concerning the custody of Jewish children cared for by non-Jewish Dutch citizens until their parents' return at the end of World War II, he wrote:

   > If I, in accord with my oath, am to implement the state's preference for serving the child's interests, my choice and decision are clear, though not, as they seldom are, easy. ... As a judge, I have to recognize as irrelevant feelings which have been aroused in me because of my childhood experiences, my own concerns

about being a parent, and my religious origins. These feelings would compel me to place the child with the biological parents, as compensation for their suffering, were it not for the guideline which stresses the child's need for continuity.

3. Justice Stewart in his dissenting opinion in *Griswold* v. *Connecticut,* 381 U.S. 479, 527 (1965) recognized the need to separate personal commitment from professional knowledge:

> Since 1879 Connecticut has had on its books a law which forbids the use of contraceptives by anyone. I think this is an uncommonly silly law. As a practical matter, the law is obviously unenforceable, except in the oblique context of the present case. As a philosophical matter, I believe the use of contraceptives in the relationship of marriage should be left to personal and private choice, based upon each individual's moral, ethical, and religious beliefs. As a matter of social policy, I think professional counsel about methods of birth control should be available to all, so that each individual's choice can be meaningfully made. But we are not asked in this case to say whether we think this law is unwise, or even asinine. We are asked to hold that it violates the United States Constitution. And that I cannot do.

See also Chief Justice Burger's opinion in *O'Connor* v. *Donaldson,* n. 13, *infra.*

4. *Beyond the Best Interests of the Child* (Epilogue, pp. 116–33).

5. See J. Goldstein, "On Being Adult and Being an Adult in Secular Law," 105 *Daedalus* 69, 71 (1976): "Unlike all other dogma, the dogma which underlies a secular legal system requires the state to tolerate any dogma unless its implementation would harm another who does not share it." See also John Ely, *Democracy and Distrust* (Cambridge, Mass.: Harvard University Press, 1980, p. 134): "One reason we have broadly based representative assemblies is to await something approaching consensus before government intervenes." Even with consensus about "scientific findings" there is the danger that they may be used in law to perpetuate grave injustices on child and family. See Stephen J. Gould, "Carrie Buck's Daughter," *Natural History*, pp. 14–18 (July 1984), reproduced in full in Appendix I. See also *Matter of Guardianship of Hayes* 608 P.2d 635 (Wash. 1980) (court addressed the question of whether it had authority to grant mother's petition for sterilization of her severely retarded sixteen-year-old daughter).

6. Testimony of Leon E. Rosenberg, M.D., Professor and Chairman, Department of Human Genetics, Yale University Medical School, before the Committee on the Judiciary, Subcommittee on Separation of Powers, U.S. Senate, Concerning the Human Life Bill (April 24, 1981).

   The problems of using scientific evidence in the legislative process were discussed by Dr. Thomas S. Kuhn, physicist and philosophy professor at Massachusetts Institute of Technology, and Dr. Joshua Lederberg, Nobel laureate in biology and President of Rockefeller University, in response to questions posed by the *New York Times:*

Q. To what extent do you think that science today has been politicized?
. . .

Dr. Kuhn: . . . There are more areas today than before where the products of research are of vast social consequence. Thus, scientists are more involved in questions with political overtones. That makes problems. One of them is public misapprehension of the extent to which expertise . . . enables a scientist to provide the concrete information called for by policymakers. . . .

Dr. Lederberg: . . . it may not be politicizing science.

Q. There is an interesting conflict here, since policymakers must pass legislation . . .

Dr. Lederberg: Yes. . . .

Q. . . . and they turn to scientists for a basis for rulemaking. But scientists don't always have the experimental data to provide such a basis. How should they deal with the legislator's demands?

Dr. Lederberg: The scientist's job is to tell them the health risks; value judgments belong to a larger sphere. That's a naive theory of separation, but it's something we ought to aspire to. *A Meeting of Biological and Philosophical Minds* (*New York Times*, March 13, 1983, p. 8E, col. 5)

7. C. E. Lindblom and D. K. Cohen, *Usable Knowledge* (New Haven and London: Yale University Press, 1979, p. 12). For a fascinating discussion on the differences between the "ordinary" observer/policymaker and the "scientific" observer/policymaker, see B. A. Ackerman, *Private Property and the Constitution,* Chapter 2 (New Haven and London: Yale University Press, 1977).

Erik Erikson, describing the nature of clinical evidence, writes of

> [the] core of *disciplined subjectivity* in clinical work which it is neither desirable nor possible altogether to replace with seemingly more objective methods. . . . It is in such apparent quicksand that we must seek the tracks of clinical evidence. No wonder that often the only clinical material which impresses some as being at all "scientific" is the evidence of the auxiliary methods of psychotherapy—neurological examination, chemical analysis, sociological study, psychological experiment, etc.—all of which derive their laws of evidence from a nonclinical field, and each of which, strictly speaking, puts the patient into nontherapeutic conditions of observation. Each of these methods may "objectify" *some* matters immensely, provide inestimable supportive evidence for *some* theories, and lead to independent methods of cure in *some* classes of patients. But it is not of the nature of the evidence provided in the psychotherapeutic encounter itself. [E. Erikson, "The Nature of Clinical Evidence," 87 *Daedalus* 65, 68, 70 (1958)]

The Supreme Court has acknowledged the special nature of clinical knowledge. In *Addington* v.

Texas, 441 U.S. 418, 430 (1979), Chief Justice Burger rejected the claim that the due process clause of the U.S. Constitution imposes a "beyond a reasonable doubt" standard on psychiatric testimony in the civil commitment of mentally ill persons. Speaking for the Court, he declined to press psychiatrists for answers beyond their competence. He observed:

> The subtleties and nuances of psychiatric diagnosis render certainties virtually beyond reach in most situations. . . . Psychiatric diagnosis . . . is to a large extent based on medical "impressions" drawn from subjective analysis and filtered through the experience of the diagnostician. . . . Within the medical discipline, the traditional standard for "factfinding" is a "reasonable medical certainty."

And in *Santosky* v. *Kramer,* 455 U.S. 745, 769 (1982), the Court considered the nature of psychiatric evidence in parental termination proceedings:

> Like civil commitment hearings, termination proceedings often require the factfinder to evaluate medical and psychiatric testimony, and to decide issues difficult to prove to a level of absolute certainty, such as lack of parental motive, absence of affection between parent and child, and failure of parental foresight and progress. . . . We hold that [a "clear and convincing evidence"] standard adequately conveys to the factfinder the level of subjective certainty about his factual conclusions necessary to satisfy due process.

8. M. Shapiro, *Law and Politics in the Supreme Court* (Glencoe: Free Press, 1964, p. 21).

See *Beyond the Best Interests of the Child* and *Before the Best Interests of the Child* on the need for and an attempt to provide more precise standards for the child placement process. But, as we cautioned in *Before the Best Interests of the Child* (p. 18): "Specificity of statutory language will never be enough. . . . Another necessary condition is that those who are empowered to intrude must understand as well as share the philosophy that underlies a policy of minimum coercive state intervention."

9. See S. Ritvo, Discussion, in J. Goldstein and J. Katz, *The Family and the Law* (New York: Free Press, 1965, p. 1032). See also our imaginary Judge Baltimore's remarks in the Dutch children's case, n. 2, *supra.*

10. Lindblom and Cohen, n. 7, *supra* at p. 13. On the rescue fantasy see *Before the Best Interests of the Child* (pp. 105, 134-36).

11. D. N. Robinson, *Psychology and Law* (New York and Oxford: Oxford University Press, 1980, pp. 26-27):

> [The] "social sciences" are not properly considered as merely the less developed version of what physics and chemistry and biology have already become. They are not, that is, "young" in the sense that time will fill them out, but different in a way that is immune to time. This is not to say that they should be accorded a lower status . . . , for to accord them a lower status is to treat them as inferior members of the same class. Instead, they form a separate class of inquiries, and the separation lingers no matter how many of the methods, concepts, or findings they might borrow from genuinely scien-

tific undertakings. If this separation is not appreciated . . . testimony generated by the "social sciences" will continue to be misused and misunderstood.

12. As do Lindblom and Cohen, we use "disciplined" (systematic) and "professional"

to separate occasional and superficially practiced activities such as classification, conceptualization, generalization, speculation, fact-gathering, and policy analysis, in which all people engage, from the presumably more sustained, elaborate, and skilled practice of these activities by professional persons bearing such designation as social scientist, statistician, systems analyst, or researcher. But we remain open to the argument that the difference is often extremely small or even nonexistent. [Lindblom and Cohen, n. 7, *supra* at p. 8, n. 11]

See also the observation of Abraham Kaplan, *The Conduct of Inquiry* (San Francisco: Chandler Publishing Co., 1964, p. 126), reproduced in Lindblom and Cohen (pp. 15–16):

Scientific observation is deliberate search, carried out with care and forethought, as contrasted with the casual and largely passive perceptions of everyday life. It is this deliberateness and control of the process of observation that is distinctive of science, not merely the use of special instruments (important as they are)—save as this use is itself indicative of forethought and care. Tycho Brahe was one of the greatest of astronomical observers though he had no telescope; Darwin also relied heavily on the naked eye; De Toqueville was a superb observer without any of the data-gathering devices of contemporary social research.

13. We agree with Chief Justice Burger's demand that judges recognize the boundaries between their professional assignment and personal beliefs: "[Judges] are not free to read their private notions of public policy or public health into the Constitution." [*O'Connor* v. *Donaldson*, 422 U.S. 563, 586 (1975) (Burger, C. J. concurring). See also Justice Stewart's dissent in *Griswold* v. *Connecticut*, n. 3, *supra*.]

CHAPTER 3: PROFESSIONAL BOUNDARIES

1. For an edited transcript of the hearing of the case and the opinion of the judge see Judith Areen, *Family Law,* pp. 429–535, 559–62 (New York: Foundation Press, 1978) (hereinafter cited as Areen, *Family Law*).

2. Areen, *Family Law* (pp. 560–61).

3. See, e.g., *Gallo* v. *Gallo,* 440 A.2d 782, 787 (Conn., 1981): "The trial court has the great advantage of hearing the witnesses and in observing their demeanor and attitudes to aid in judging the credibility of testimony." And see 3A Wigmore, *Evidence* §946 (Chadbourne rev., 1970): "The demeanor of the witness on the stand may always be considered by the jury in their estimation of his credibility."

Using a witness's demeanor in evaluating his testimony is not equivalent to judging his character. See, e.g., *Kovacs* v. *Szentes,* 130 Conn. 229, 233, 33 A.2d 124, 126 (1943):

> "[The] trier's right to take into account its ob-
> servation of the demeanor of witnesses is lim-
> ited to the observation of such genuine and
> spontaneous reactions by them in the court-
> room as bear upon the credibility to be ac-
> corded to their testimony given under oath.
> . . ." Some of these findings [e.g., the wife found
> to be "under the domination of the defendant"]
> went beyond any question of credibility of wit-
> nesses . . . [and so constituted] error.

4. Areen, *Family Law* (pp. 559–62).

5. *Garska* v. *McCoy,* 278 S.E.2d 357, 361 (W.Va. 1981).

6. *Id.* at 361–63 (1981). The Connecticut Supreme Court
   has apparently seen less need for statutory presumptions than the West Virginia court did in *Garska* v.
   McCoy. In response to the allegation that the divorce
   custody statute was unconstitutionally vague because of its failure to provide guidelines for trial
   judges more specific than the "best interest" standard, the Connecticut Supreme Court said:

   > We continue to adhere to the view that the leg-
   > islature was acting wisely in leaving the deli-
   > cate and difficult process of fact-finding in
   > family matters to flexible, individualized adju-
   > dication of the particular facts of each case
   > without the constraint of objective guidelines.
   > [*Seymour* v. *Seymour,* 180 Conn. 705, 710
   > (1980)]

   The court recognized, however, the difficulties of making assessments of comparative fitness. It dismissed
   the contention that the trial court abused its discre-

tion by giving insufficient weight to evidence concerning the parenting abilities of the father and of the mother, and excessive weight to identification of the child's primary psychological parent:

> Once it is definitively established, as it was here, that each parent is loving, caring and otherwise entirely suitable, the court perforce must look to other factors to come to a decision about custody. The court was not in error in basing its award of custody to the mother on her strong and healthy relationship to her daughter, her willingness and ability to devote time to her daughter, and her willingness to facilitate visitation by the father. [*Id.* at 713]

The trial court had relied on the testimony of one of three experts, whose opinion conflicted with that of the other two. The Connecticut Supreme Court indicated that trial judges ought to be cautious in weighing expert testimony:

> The appellants challenge not only the concept of the psychological parent but also the methodology of the psychiatrist who presented the concept to the court. The weight to be given to psychological testimony by professionals in mental health is, in matters of custody, as it is elsewhere, a question for the trier of fact. It should be noted, however, that expert opinion must be evaluated in light of the expert's opportunity to come to a reasoned conclusion. . . . As this case illustrates, long-range forecasts about future child development are sometimes based upon relatively few and brief interviews and tests conducted under circumstances of

stress. It is not clear to what extent the analytic insights derived from long and intensive psychotherapy can readily be translated into an evaluative setting that is governed by a radically different time frame. [*Id.* at 712–13]

7. See *Beyond the Best Interests of the Child* (p. 175, n. 12). Such a situation does not justify postponing a decision for two years—as happened in a case in which one of the authors gave testimony—in the hope that enough could be learned to render a decision that would truly be in the children's best interests. The judge should have recognized the immediate threat posed to the children by this period of uncertainty.

8. 9 Wigmore, *Evidence* §2569 (Chadbourne rev., 1970). Wigmore goes on to say:

The dilemma sometimes . . . has given rise to much discussion over extreme cases—particularly the celebrated problem once put by a King of England, whether a judge could lawfully respite a convicted person whom he personally knew to be innocent. But it is now well enough understood that there is no impracticable dilemma. If the judge, as a man and an observer, has any personal knowledge, he may (and sometimes morally must) utilize it by taking the stand as a witness and telling in that capacity what he knows . . . ; this solves the dilemma without either injuring justice or violating principle.

For an interesting analogy see the provisions of the *Administrative Procedure Act* concerning "official notice." If an agency proposes to take judicial notice, it must inform the parties and give them a chance for rebuttal, 5 U.S.C. §556(e) (1977).

9. Areen, *Family Law* (p. 561). See also *In re Ross*, 29 Ill.App.3d 157 (1975):

> This is an appeal of Elaine Ross and Susan Ross, minors, from a custody decision of the Circuit Court . . . by which it was determined that the minors, Elaine Ross and Susan Ross, should be returned to their natural parents. The basis of the decision was founded upon the finding that the children had been physically and emotionally neglected while in the care of their foster parents. [*Id.* at 158]

> * * *

> The trial court interviewed Elaine and Susan in chambers . . . at the request of the parties. . . . The trial court stated that both girls . . . expressed strong desires to remain with the Reeves. . . . The trial judge also revealed that he had given both girls the "house-tree-person" psychological test previously given by Dr. McBride because he questioned some of Dr. McBride's conclusions. The court, however, would not discuss the results of the tests. [*Id.* at 166]

> * * *

> We have been directed to no evidence of any neglect of the children by Mrs. Reeves, and the conclusion of the trial court as to this issue

appears to be unsupported in the record. [*Id.* at 167]

* * *

It is the general rule that all court proceedings which are the basis of a judgment or order should be set forth in the record so that a court of review may make an informed and intelligent resolution of the issues on appeal. We also recognize, however, the nature of custody cases, and the often bitter and emotional atmosphere which surrounds them, so that a trial court must have some discretion as to interviewing the children in the privacy of the court chambers. [*Id.* at 170]

* * *

[The] trial court did reveal substantive portions of the interview, except for the results of the "house-tree-person" tests. . . . Apparently the trial court felt qualified to question and analyze the testimony of psychologists. It may very well be that the trial court was so qualified, but such separate testing and conclusions derived therefrom not shown of record would require reversal. It is not good practice for a court to undertake independently, any such analysis. A court should review and decide a case only on the basis of the record. . . .

The trial court here questioned the competence or conclusions of psychological tests

placed in evidence. Apparently the court undertook the "house-tree-person" tests independently and came to certain conclusions as the
result of such private testing. Such procedure
was not proper. All conclusions should be based
upon evidence properly introduced in open
court and subject to cross-examination and
questioning by the parties or their counsel. Under the circumstances, any circuit judge who
now proceeds in this case should not be involved in such testing, since it could be con-
tended that the court might base a decision on
factors which are not made part of the record.
This cause should, therefore, proceed, upon remand, before a trial judge other than the judge
who conducted the proceedings from which the
present appeal was taken. [*Id.* at 171]

10. The judge-as-witness issue, though it may seem obvious, was not perceived by one of the authors who
testified at the trial and who served as a consultant
to counsel for Steven in preparing his appeal. He was
preoccupied with focusing appellate review on the trial
court's failure to apply the continuity principle and
the presumption in favor of the primary caregiver and
never thought to raise this alternative basis for reversal. Nor did the appellate court on its own address
the matter in its opinion affirming the trial court. *Rose*
v. *Rose,* Areen, *Family Law* (pp. 561–62). See also *Rea*
v. *Rea,* 195 Or. 252, 245 P.2d 884 (1952), especially the
concurrence of Judge Latourette explaining that "a
child custody case cannot be decided on evidence de
hors the record" (*id.* at 897). See also other cases cited
in 9 Wigmore, *Evidence* §2569 (Chadbourne rev.,
1970).

11. *Kovacs* v. *Szentes,* 130 Conn. 229, 233, 33A.2d 124, 126 (1943). See also Guggenheim, "The Right to Be Represented but Not Heard: Reflections on Legal Representation for Children," 59 *New York University Law Review* 76, 102–103 (1984).

> [A] critical difference in the role played by lawyers [as champions advocating their *personal* views of best interest] and psychiatrists and other experts in cases involving children [is that] expert witnesses are subject to cross examination by the other party's counsel. Under a skillful cross examination, the expert's knowledge and competence will be tested, and his prejudices and biases, if he has any, will be revealed to the fact-finder. [*Id.* at 103]

12. *Rose* v. *Rose,* Areen, *Family Law,* 1983 Supp. (p. 104). On the basis of uncontradicted expert testimony the judge found:

> Jason is emotionally unstable and depressed beyond that to be expected from a child his age. . . . [Diane] became inclined toward periods of wide emotional swings. At times she would become enraged. Though this was probably not directed at Jason in a physical sense, he did have to experience it. She sometimes sank into depression, at other times acted more like the child's friend than mother, and then could swing into an aggressive mood. . . . [She] became unstable. I think Jason suffered from this inconsistency as much as from the frequent visitations. . . . [Steven] was more consistent in his parenting of Jason. . . . Above all, he has been a good father to Jason on a consistent basis.

The judge then observed that the history of Jason's relationship with his parents meant that less weight should be given in this case to the "continuity of care, stability, and psychological parenthood [that] go hand in hand with the in-custody parent." "There is," he said, "less continuity to be disturbed, little stability, and no single psychological parent." And he concluded that Diane was disqualified—unfit—to be the custodial parent and that "Jason's best interest lies with his father as primary custodian. He is more stable and offers Jason the best chance to make progress towards normalcy" (*id.* at 104–105).

13. *Id.* at 103, 104.

14. On the role of judges in medical decisions, see *Before the Best Interests of the Child* (pp. 91–111). See especially the discussion of Judge Elwyn's decision in *In Re Sampson,* *id.* at 101–105.

    For another example of a judge's using courtroom observations as a basis for making a custody award, see *In the marriage of Sampson, J. J. and Sampson, J. M.,* Family Court of Australia at Melbourne, (1977) FLC 90-253, p. 76, 355. In this case Justice Fogarty ordered that custody of a four-year-old boy (whose parents had separated before his birth and who had always lived with his mother) be awarded to his father. The decision turned on the judge's perception of the character of the paternal grandmother, Mrs. Sampson:

> I do not regard the father as a highly attractive alternative. Were it not for the presence of his mother in this case I think it almost inevitable that the result would and must have been the

reverse. I have great confidence in Mrs. Sampson as a surrogate mother of this child. She struck me both in these proceedings and in the previous ones as representing all that one could really ask for in a difficult case of this sort. I feel that if anybody is going to help this child along the road it can only be Mrs. Sampson assisting her son. [*Id.* at 76, 367]

Justice Fogarty had found the child's father (Mrs. Sampson's son) to suffer from "defects of personality and character," but said about his mother, Mrs. Sampson (the child's grandmother):

It sometimes happens that when one sees again a witness in the witness box after a gap one forms a differing impression, but in this case Mrs. Sampson impressed me just as much on this occasion as she did on the past occasion. It was not just her manner or style of answering questions or indeed their content when the transcript is read. What was significant was that she exuded a rather down-to-earth relaxed commonsense approach and certainly gave a heartening impression of a woman perfectly capable of meeting troubles and dealing with them as best she could. [*Id.* at 76, 361]

Though a psychologist and the Family Court Counsellor had provided Justice Fogarty with their assessments of the characters of the child's mother and father as they related to their ability to be good parents to the child, he had been provided with no such assessment of the grandmother and relied solely on his own observations.

15. 84 Ill.App.3d 901, 405 N.E.2d 1289 (1980). The child's name is not given in the report of the case. We call her Rachel.

16. *Id.* at 906, 405 N.E.2d at 1293. The statutory provisions are reproduced in the opinion.

17. *Id.* at 903–904, 405 N.E.2d at 1291.

18. *Id.* at 904, 405 N.E.2d at 1292 (emphasis added).

19. On appeal the trial judge's visitation order was reversed because he had not made the explicit threshold finding of serious endangerment that was required by the statute. *In re Marriage of Solomon,* 84 Ill.App.3d 901, 907, 405 N.E.2d 1289, 1293 (1980). See *Before The Best Interests of the Child* (pp. 75–77) on the lack of consensus about the meaning and specific cause(s) of serious emotional damage. It may be that such statutes press experts in child development to answer questions that they cannot answer and to which their response should be either "I don't know" or "I don't understand the question."

    On our views concerning court-mandated visits see *Beyond the Best Interests of the Child* (Epilogue, pp. 116–33).

20. See also *Schottenstein* v. *Schottenstein,* 384 So.2d 933, 936 (Fla.App. 1980), in which the appellate court vacated the trial court's order for psychiatric counseling in a custody case. It said: "We have searched the record to determine the basis for the trial court's decision. Interspersed with colloquy bearing on varied subjects, we find this:"

Mr. Schottenstein: ... I have a concern that they will have too much money. I want them to grow up to have a right sense of values. ... If anything, they have too much money and they should learn to handle it better.

The Court: There are problems and there are problems. Maybe there is too much money. I have seen very wealthy children end up in dope and kill themselves.

* * *

I believe in psychologists and I believe in psychiatrists. If you want you make the children go.

* * *

They are smart children and let's get this resolved.

Do the children come back upset after they visit with him?

Ms. Schottenstein: Sometimes.

The Court: Doesn't that indicate to you the children ought to talk to a professional?

How many fathers do they have? If the children are upset, *I think they should talk to a professional.*

The appellate court then observed: "While the trial judge may be a proselyte of psychological evaluations and consultation for every minor child of divorced parents, we cannot ignore the countervailing right of a person to be free from a compulsory mental examination" *(ibid.).*

21. For a detailed discussion of the lawyer's role in representing children, see *Before the Best Interests of the Child* (pp. 111–29). See also Chapter 5, *infra.*

22. Anna Freud, "On the Difficulties of Communicating with Children," in J. Goldstein and J. Katz, *The Family and the Law* (New York: Free Press, 1965, pp. 261–62).

23. See excerpt from *Addington* v. *Texas,* n. 36, *infra.*

24. For a confusing view, see Michael E. Radin, "The Role of the Lawyer for the Preschool Child in Custody Litigation," *Journal of Psychiatry & Law* 431 (Winter 1981). Radin is apparently aware, *in theory,* of the boundaries which exist between the lawyer for children and the specialist in child development and mental health. While occasionally sensitive to these boundaries, he often seems to be proposing that the lawyer *in practice* ignore them.

25. As the *Rose, Solomon,* and *Stone* cases illustrate, judges and lawyers sometimes trespass into the child development field, perhaps because this discipline deals with universal human experiences. They forget, as did the dissenting judge in *Adoption of Randolph,* 68 Wisc.2d 64, 79, 227 N.W.2d 634, 640 (1974), that their decisionmaking authority does not rest on their personal opinions. In that case the Wisconsin Supreme Court affirmed a trial court's denial of an adoption petition by the grandparents of two children who had been in the care of another relative since the death

of their parents. A psychiatrist had testified at the trial that if the children were to be separated from this relative, "what one might reasonably anticipate is regression in behavior: potty training, night bedwetting, thumb sucking, trauma, and tantrums, more aggressiveness" (*id.* at 72, 227 N.W.2d at 638). The dissenting judge said: "Anyone familiar with small children knows that this type of separation trauma is of short duration and had children of this age been with others than their parents because of the parents' temporary inability to care for them . . . it would be a rare case where a court would say, 'You have been away for 20 months; you can't have your children!' " (*id.* at 79, 227 N.W.2d at 642). This judge obscured the question of whether he was qualified to render an opinion about the significance of separation trauma by his opening phrase "Anyone familiar with small children knows. . . . "

26. *Report of the Committee of Inquiry into the Death of Maria Colwell* 59, 60, 67 (1974), reprinted in *Before the Best Interests of the Child* (Appendix I, pp. 157–58, 161).

27. See Chapter 2 *supra.*

28. In certain contexts, there may be special temptations for experts to go beyond their competence. See Lyon and Levine, "Ethics, Power, and Advocacy," 6 *Law and Human Behavior* 65, 73 (1982):

> The psychologist may deal with requests for prediction and treatment by taking a stance of scientific purity and refusing to perform requested tasks because of the limitations on his expertise. The psychologist who does so, how-

ever, is unlikely to remain employed in the criminal justice system. The individual psychologist thus may confront both an ethical dilemma and personal financial distress.

29. James and Joyce Robertson, "The Psychological Parent," 87 *Adoption & Fostering* 19, 21–22 (Issue #1, 1977). See also *Before the Best Interests of the Child* (pp. 39–57) on longtime caretakers.

30. See Anna Freud, "On the Difficulties of Communicating with Children," n. 22, *supra*.

31. *The Emotional Needs of Infants and Young Children: Implication for Policy and Practice* (ed. Graham Martin. Adelaide, South Australia: The Association for the Welfare of Children in Hospital, 1979, p. 251). Words in brackets were added by the Robertsons (London, July 1, 1982).

32. *Id.* at 251. Words in brackets added by the Robertsons (London, July 1, 1982).

33. *Id.* at 251–52. Words in brackets added by the Robertsons (London, July 1, 1982).

34. *Beyond the Best Interests of the Child* (p. 66). See *Lehman* v. *Lycoming County Children's Services Agency,* 458 U.S. 502, 514 n. 18 (1982): "There is also the danger that 'if litigation expenses mount, social workers and charitable organizations . . . may well become less willing to seek placements for children over their parents' objections, whether rational or irrational, even though in their honest judgment the child's best interests demand it' (*Sylvander* v. *New England Home for Little Wanderers,* 584 F.2d, at 1112)."

35. *Bennett* v. *Jeffreys* 387 N.Y.S.2d 821, 827 (1976). But see *Hoy* v. *Willis* 165 N.J. Super. 265 (1978) in which an appellate court overturned a trial judge's rejection of "unquestioned, uncontradicted and unrefuted" expert testimony. The trial judge was put off by the expert's answer to a hypothetical question (posed by the judge) that was irrelevant to the facts of the case.

> That question was:
>> "If a couple kidnapped an infant, kept it for four years, and within that four years they became the psychological parents of the child and if both the parents and the kidnappers were equal in all respect would it be in the best interest of the child to continue custody with the kidnappers?"
>
> Dr. Hollander answered that question in the affirmative. In a letter opinion dated September 5, 1978 the trial judge, in commenting on this answer of the doctor, said:
>> "This Court finds it impossible to accept this line of reasoning. Unfortunately the court must either disbelieve the only expert opinion before it or by accepting it, decide that as a matter of law, the best interest of the child must give way to the rights of the parent to custody of her child."
>
> * * *
>
> It is clear to us that the trial judge failed to recognize and apply present-day concepts of

psychological parentage in resolving the custody issue before him. We would normally remand a case of this nature to the trial judge for reconsideration and the application of appropriate legal principles. We are persuaded, however, to exercise our original jurisdiction, . . . make our own findings and bring the litigation to a conclusion for two reasons. First, the litigation involves the custody of the very young and has already been pending without resolution entirely too long. Second, since the evidence is virtually undisputed, the observation of a trial judge on matters of credibility and demeanor are not of crucial significance. [*Id.* at 270, 276–77]

36. In another context, see *Addington* v. *Texas,* 441 U.S. 418, 429 (1979): "Whether the individual is mentally ill and dangerous to either himself or others and is in need of confined therapy turns on the *meaning* of the facts which must be interpreted by expert psychiatrists and psychologists."

37. See Chapter 2.

38. *Beyond the Best Interests of the Child* (Epilogue, p. 114).

CHAPTER 4: CROSSING PROFESSSIONAL BORDERS

1. Civil Action H–75–18, U.S. District Ct., District of Conn., February 2, 1982 (Zampano, J.). The children, then ages four and six, had been placed in another foster home.

2. The child's rights are traditionally of secondary concern when courts fashion remedies to right wrongs toward parents by agents of the state. See Note, "A Damages Remedy for Abuses by Child Protection Workers," 90 *Yale Law Journal* 681 (1981). This is not true in most other cases; see *Before the Best Interests of the Child* (p. 57). "Historically, damages have been regarded as the ordinary remedy for an invasion of personal interests in liberty." *Bivens* v. *Six Unknown Federal Narcotics Agents,* 403 U.S. 388, 395 (1970).

3. Memorandum in Opposition to Motion to Dismiss, *Rivera* v. *Marcus,* Civil Action H–75–18, U.S. District Ct., District of Conn., May 21, 1980.

4. The appellate judge went further than the district judge. He affirmed that there had been a violation of constitutional rights and ordered a hearing on the remedy. He stated: "The years which have passed since the . . . children were removed from the [first foster] home will militate against their removal from the home of the present foster parents at any future hearing." *Rivera* v. *Marcus,* 696 F.2d 1016, 1025 n.12 (2d Cir. 1982). The appellate judge did not reach this conclusion on the basis of testimony from experts in child development. Nor did he disclose any acquired knowledge from this field or identify statutory or case law upon which he might have relied in order to reach this determination on his own.

   For another view on using the placement of children as a remedy or as punishment for adults see *Bennett* v. *Jeffreys,* 387 N.Y.S.2d 821, 827 (1976). In that case, acting on his general knowledge of a child's need for continuity, Judge Breitel observed: "The resolution of cases must not provide incentives for those likely to take the law into their own hands. Thus, those who obtain custody of children unlawfully, particularly by kidnapping, violence, or flight from the jurisdiction of the courts, must be deterred. Society may not reward, except at its peril, the lawless because the passage of time has made correction inexpedient. Yet, even then, circumstances may require that, in the best interests of the child, the unlawful acts be blinked."

5. *Ross* v. *Hoffman,* 364 A.2d 596, 598, 599 (Md. 1976).

6. *Id.* at 599–600 (emphasis supplied).

7. See also *Powers* v. *Haddan,* 353 A.2d 641 (Md. 1976), which was handed down after the chancellor reached his decision and Mrs. Ross had relied upon it. The *Powers* court observed:

> The presumption that a parent should have custody of his or her child is not based upon sympathetic concern for the parent nor upon parental *rights.* This presumption is a judicial device which shifts the burden of proof to the nonparent seeking custody and recognizes that the child's best interest is usually served in the custody of its natural parents:
>
>> "Where parents claim the custody of a child, there is a *prima facie* presumption that the child's welfare will be best subserved in the care and custody of its parents rather than in the custody of others, and the burden is then cast upon the parties opposing them to show the contrary." [Citation omitted]

*   *   *

[A] long period of separation serves merely to rebut the presumption in favor of parental custody. It does not require that custody *not* be awarded the parent. [*Id.* at 645–46; emphasis in original]

The intermediate appellate court in *Ross* v. *Hoffman*, n. 5 *supra* at 598–99, noted that the chancellor "cited many of the cases upon which we relied in *Powers*, and expressly recognized that the Hoffmans had the burden of overcoming the natural parent presumption." The court went on:

Perhaps appellant's misinterpretation of *Powers* lies in the sense of rigidity, if not conclusiveness, with which the term "presumption" is viewed. Too often those skilled at law treat all presumptions as decisive irrespective of the evidence, and fail to recognize that for the most part they are merely guidelines by which to reason, conclusive only in the absence of evidence to the contrary, and are aught but one more auncel weight in the judicial balance. In the natural parent context it is nothing more than a burden-placing device. It puts the burden of persuasion on the nonbiological "parent" and is overcome when sufficient evidence is introduced and believed by the trier of fact to convince him that the child's best interest will be served by one other than a natural parent. [*Id.* at 600]

8. *Bennett* v. *Jeffreys*, 387 N.Y.S.2d 821, 829 (Fuchsberg, J. concurring) (1976). See *Petition of New England Home for Little Wanderers*, 328 N.E.2d 854, 861 (Mass. 1975):

> In invoking the "best interests of the child,"
> the Legislature did not intend to disregard the
> ties between the child and its natural parent, or
> to threaten a satisfactory family with loss of
> children because by reason of temporary ad-
> versity they are placed in foster care. A parent
> cannot be deprived unless some affirmative
> reason is shown for doing so such as a finding
> . . . of a separation so long as to permit very
> strong bonds to develop between the child and
> the prospective adoptive parents.

See also note 18, *infra.*

9. *Ross* v. *Hoffman,* 364 A.2d 596, 599 (1976).

10. *Id.* at 600. See also Jane W. Ellis, "Evaluating the
Expert: Judicial Expectations of Expert Opinion Evidence in Child Placement Adjudications," 5 *Cardozo
Law Review* 587, n. 61, 606–607 (1984):
　　"A perusal of cases in which legislative facts
from *Beyond the Best Interests of the Child* . . . have
been accepted as standards for defining 'best interests' indicates that a number of different techniques
have been employed. One court took formal judicial
notice of the work. See *In re Adoption of Michelle Lee
T.,* 44 Cal.App.3d 699, 706, 117 Cal.Rptr. 856, 859–60
(Dist. Ct. App. 1975) (taking 'judicial notice of a re-
cent authoritative work on child placement, cited by
the Supreme Court of California in *In re B.G.* [11
Cal.3d 679, 523 P.2d 244, 114 Cal.Rptr. 444 (1974)]').
Others have taken what appears to be informal judicial notice, ostensibly proceeding *sua sponte* to discuss the book and apply it to the case. See, e.g., *In re
Mendas,* 104 Misc.2d 357, 362, 428 N.Y.S.2d 419, 422

(Fam. Ct. 1980); *In re Samantha S.*, 80 Misc.2d 217, 219, 362 N.Y.S.2d 921, 923 (Fam. Ct. 1974); *Nathan & Cathy M.* v. *Catholic Guardian Society*, 76 Misc.2d 1003, 1005–1006, 352 N.Y.S.2d 319, 322 (Fam. Ct. 1973). Courts have accepted the expert facts when introduced into evidence by a party. See, e.g., *In re Adoption of B. by E. & R.*, 152 N.J. Super. 546, 556, 378 A.2d 90, 95 (Union County Ct. 1977) ('Based upon theories articulated by Goldstein, Freud, and Solnit in . . . *Beyond the Best Interests of the Child*, . . . E. and R. persuasively argue that a removal of B. from his present home would be detrimental. . . . '). One court cited the book in a long string of cases without indicating that it represented a form of authority distinguishable from case law. *Rodriguez* v. *Koschny*, 57 Ill.App.3d 355, 362, 373 N.E.2d 47, 52 (1978). Courts may rely, in traditional common law fashion, on a reference to the book in other cases or in other jurisdictions. See, e.g., *New Jersey Div. of Youth & Family Servs.* v. *Huggins*, 148 N.J. Super. 86, 94, 371 A.2d 841, 845 (Camden County Ct. 1977). In *In re Patricia Ann W.*, 89 Misc.2d 368, 375, 392 N.Y.S.2d 180, 185 (Fam. Ct. 1977), the law regarding the effect of biological versus 'psychological parentage' is traced, and the court not only refers to the book, but mentions in a footnote the fact that 'there is no doubt that our late colleague, Judge Zukerman, would wish to be remembered as the forward looking jurist so far ahead of his time whose pioneer judicial recognition of the psychological parent school of thought ultimately became the law of this State' (*id.* at 375 n.*, 392 N.Y.S.2d at 185 n.*). Judge Zukerman's 'landmark opinion' was *In re Catherine S.*, 74 Misc.2d 154, 347 N.Y.S.2d 470 (Fam. Ct. 1973). See also *New Jersey Div. of Youth & Family Servs.* v. *B.W.*, 157 N.J. Super. 301, 304, 384

A.2d 923, 925 (Camden County Ct. 1977) ('psychological parenthood' is becoming a widely recognized and important factor in determining custody based on the best interest of the child)."

11. *Ross* v. *Hoffman* 372 A.2d 582, 593–94 (Md. 1977), citing *Bennett* v. *Jeffreys*, 387 N.Y.S.2d 821, 827, 356 N.E.2d 277, 283 (1976).

12. *Id.* at 593, 594 (1977). The court applied the criteria to the facts of the case at hand:

> The chancellor could properly find the existence of exceptional circumstances which would make custody in the mother detrimental to the best interest of the child from the protracted separation of mother from child, beginning at the child's tender age of about four months and lasting for eight and a half years, combined with the strong attachment of the child to the custodian, the emotional reaction of the child to the dispute over her custody and the possible emotional effect on her if the change were made, the uncertainty of the stability of the mother's household in light of her marriage, the lapse of some eight years before the mother attempted to reclaim the child, the questions as to the real motive of the mother in seeking reclamation and as to the genuineness of her desire to have the custody of her daughter. There being exceptional circumstances rebutting the presumption that custody in the mother was in the best interest of the child, the chancellor properly considered who should be awarded custody in order to subserve the child's best interest. [*Id.* at 594]

And see *D.* v. *M.*, 3 All E.R. 897 (1982) in which Lord Justice Ormrod declared that generally accepted special knowledge from child development about continuity had by 1982 become a part of English custody law through precedent. Reversing a lower court's order to transfer a child from his mother to his long absent father, he stated:

> [It] is generally accepted by those who are professionally concerned with children that, particularly in the early years, continuity of care is the most important part of a child's sense of security and that disruption of established bonds is to be avoided whenever it is possible to do so. Where, as in this case, a child of two years of age has been brought up without interruption by the mother (or a mother substitute) it should not be removed from her care unless there are strong countervailing reasons for doing so. This is not only the professional view, it is commonly accepted in all walks of life, and was the recommendation of the experienced welfare officer. [*Id.* at 902–903]

See also *Lehman* v. *Lycoming County Children's Services*, 458 U.S. 502 (1982) in which the Supreme Court declined to permit the use of federal habeas corpus to give Federal courts jurisdiction to hear reargument of final state court decisions to terminate parental rights. Justice Powell for the Court said:

> The State's interest in finality is unusually strong in child custody disputes. The grant of federal habeas would prolong uncertainty for children such as the Lehman sons, possibly lessening their chances of adoption. It is undis-

puted that children require secure, stable, long-term, continuous relationships with their parents or foster parents. There is little that can be as detrimental to a child's sound development as uncertainty over whether he is to remain in his current "home," under the care of his parents or foster parents, especially when such uncertainty is prolonged. Extended uncertainty would be inevitable in many cases if federal courts had jurisdiction to relitigate state custody decisions. [*Id.* at 513–14]

13. *Ross* v. *Hoffman*, 364 A.2d 596, 601–602 (1976). See *Before the Best Interests of the Child* (pp. 39–57, 194–95) on how time might be fixed for statutory purposes with special provision in certain cases for the use of expert testimony.

14. Or. Rev. Stat. §107.137 (1981). "None of these factors are to be considered in isolation or to the exclusion of the others" (*ibid.*).

15. *Ibid.* (emphasis supplied).

16. *Derby* v. *Derby,* 31 Or.App. 803, 806–807, 571 P.2d 562, 564 (1977), modified on other grounds, 31 Or.App. 1333, 572 P.2d 1080 (1977), *reh'g den.* 281 Or. 323 (1979). "No preference in custody shall be given to the mother over the father for the sole reason that she is the mother." Or. Rev. Stat. §107.137 (3) (1981).

17. For another, albeit less sharply focused, example, see Mich. C.L.A. §722.23 (1984), which lists several factors to be considered in determining the custody of a child:

(a) The love, affection, and other emotional ties existing between the parties involved and the child.

(b) The capacity and disposition of the parties involved to give the child love, affection, and guidance and continuation of the educating and raising of the child in its religion or creed, if any.

(c) The capacity and disposition of the parties involved to provide the child with food, clothing, medical care, or other remedial care recognized and permitted under the laws of this state in place of medical care, and other material needs.

(d) The length of time the child has lived in a stable, satisfactory environment, and the desirability of maintaining continuity.

(e) The permanence, as a family unit, of the existing or proposed custodial home or homes.

(f) The moral fitness of the parties involved.

(g) The mental and physical health of the parties involved.

(h) The home, school, and community record of the child.

(i) The reasonable preference of the child, if the court deems the child to be of sufficient age to express preference.

(j) The willingness and ability of each of the parents to facilitate and encourage a close and continuing parent–child relationship between the child and the other parent.

(k) Any other factor considered by the court to be relevant to a particular child custody dispute.

18. Similarly, were the guidelines to disposition proposed in *Beyond the Best Interests of the Child* and the grounds for intervention proposed in *Before the Best Interests of the Child* incorporated in legislation or judicial precedent, some knowledge from child development would become part of the professional equipment of law-trained persons. These guidelines and grounds "incorporate principles of general application that have been distilled from psychoanalytic theory and from an extensive body of diagnostic and therapeutic work in child development" (*Before the Best Interests of the Child*, n.13, pp. 228–29). Courts would no longer need to have individual clinical examinations in order to make a finding that enforced separation of a four-year-old from the only parent he has known will have serious repercussions for his development; or that a child's absent biological parent cannot, by virtue of blood ties alone, replace a long-time caregiver as psychological parent; or that a murderous parental attack on a child will destroy the possibility of his feeling safe again in the care of that parent; or that a child's capacity to develop meaningful relationships will be undermined if he is forced to maintain contact with separated parents who are not in general agreement about visits. These guidelines and grounds thus identify situations in which judges and lawyers representing children may cross professional borders.

19. W. Va. Code §48-2-15 (1980).

20. *Garska* v. *McCoy*, 278 S.E.2d 357, 363 (W. Va. 1981).

21. *Id.* at 364.

22. A. B. Arons, "Achieving Wider Scientific Literacy,"
Daedalus, 91 (Spring 1983). Arons' argument that science should be taught in a historical and intellectual
context rather than as "the mere assertion of end results" (*id.* at 105) led to our thinking about statutes
and precedents in this fashion.

See also Henry M. Hart and John T. Mc-
Naughton, "Evidence and Inference in Law," 87 *Daedalus*, 40–64 (Winter 1958):

> [The] law has no single technique for connect-
> ing its conclusions with supporting data.
>
> *   *   *
>
> Legal directions always contemplate the sub-
> suming of particulars under previously estab-
> lished generals. Their application always
> involves the double task of ascertaining the
> general which is to be applied and of identify-
> ing the particulars which make it applicable. In
> few, if any, other disciplines is a problem of this
> dual type encountered. In most other disci-
> plines, the generalizations are drawn from the
> facts and are controlled by them. The general-
> izations of the law, in contrast, are prescriptive
> rather than descriptive. [*Id.* at 40–41]
>
> The facts which guide judgment about
> whether an indeterminate standard should be
> particularized in the form of a technical rule for
> certain classes of cases . . . are not facts about
> a particular event which bear upon the question
> whether that event should be subsumed under,
> or brings into play, a general direction or law.

Rather they are facts which bear upon the question whether a general proposition of law should be formulated in one way or another. They concern not particular happenings but general behavior and the general tendencies, consequences, and evaluation of behavior. They are "legislative," as distinguished from adjudicative, facts. They are facts, correspondingly, which are of concern to many who are not parties to the litigation and which ought not to be left to be settled solely under the aegis of the adversaries before the court.

Legislatures, of course, consider facts of this kind in deciding whether to enact a statute. So do courts in formulating grounds of decision. There are differences, however: *first,* the court is concerned with such facts only to the extent necessary to formulate a just ground for the decision of the controversy before it, and, *second,* the court is under the necessity of relating the ground of decision which it formulates in some rational fashion to the underlying direction which it is elaborating, and hence is specially concerned with facts which help it to do this. [*Id.* at 54–55]

What rules, then, do apply? What techniques does the law follow?

*   *   *

[These] are among the most neglected questions of legal scholarship.

*   *   *

At the root of the superficially strange neglect of problems of how legislative facts are to be determined by a court is the traditional reluctance of the courts to admit that they are making law at all. Yet make law they do, although it is interstitial, elaborative law, made or supposed to be made under the discipline of an effort to show or be able to show a reasoned connection between the newly made law and established doctrines of law which underlie and justify it. In the making of this law the courts have constant need of knowledge to inform and guide their judgment.

The need for knowledge is occasionally met by expert testimony. . . . Receipt of testimony of this kind is by no means uncommon, although the difference between expert testimony offered to prove the happening or non-happening of an historical event and expert testimony offered to guide the court in its elaboration of law is not always noted. [*Id.* at 55–56]

A legislature, unlike a court, is free from the necessity of relating its determinations, by some process of reasoning, to principles and policies or standards already settled into the law. Within the broad limits set by constitutional restraints, it can make a new social policy, if this seems to be the wise thing to do; and, if necessary, it can create new institutional structures to carry out the policy. This it can do with full representation and full opportunity for hearing of all the interests affected. . . . Here then, it might seem, is the point of decision at which not only scientific investigation but sci-

entific determination could be most profitably
employed in the law. [*Id.* at 57]

23. Courts have recognized that these presumptive preferences (for natural parents) can be overturned if applying them would ill-serve the child's need for
continuity of care. The protection of continuity is one
of the functions which the presumptions were intended to serve.

In an 1889 case, long before the notion of continuity was formulated by experts in child development, the Court of Error and Appeals in New Jersey
recognized that the judge's task was to "fix the future
status of the child [Clara] with some stability and permanence" and that her welfare required that she be
allowed to remain with her long-term foster parents
rather than be forced, as the lower court had decreed,
to live with her natural parents. *Richard* v. *Collins*, 17
A.831, 832 (N.J. 1889). Although biological parents
were presumptively favored at the time, the court declared:

> Nature's provision of mutual affection com-
> monly exists as the incentive to parental and
> filial duty and the bond of family union. It is
> the instinct of childhood to attach itself and
> cling to those who perform towards it the pa-
> rental office, and they become endeared to it by
> the ministering to its dependence. . . . In a con-
> troversy over its possession, its welfare will be
> the paramount consideration in controlling the
> discretion of the court. [*Ibid.*]

And in overturning the presumption, the court explicitly identified those functions of natural parents which
the foster parents had assumed in this case.

They agreed to take it and rear it as their own child. They nursed and cared for it through helpless infancy. They watched over and provided for it as it grew in years. Whatever it has known of parental love and care is from them. It would be passing strange if it had not become bound to them, and the home they gave it, with a child's affection. They . . . are still willing and abundantly able to provide for it, and advance it in life. [*Id.* at 833]

Because the mechanical application of the presumption would not serve its purpose, the court was willing to overturn it. In an earlier case, the Supreme Court of Kansas overturned the presumption in favor of fathers, after recognizing that evidence of the past performance of the parents and foster parents was the best guide to determine the custody of the child.

The right of the father must be considered; the right of the one who has filled the parental place for years should be considered. Perhaps it may not be technically correct to speak of that as a right; and yet, they who have for years filled the place of the parent, have discharged all the obligations of care and support, and especially when they have discharged these duties during those years of infancy when the burden is especially heavy, when the labor and care are of a kind whose value cannot be expressed in money—when all these labors have been performed and the child has bloomed into bright and happy girlhood, it is but fair and proper that their previous faithfulness, and the interest and affection which these labors have created in them, should be respected. Above all things, the paramount consideration is, what will promote the welfare of the child?

* * *

What the future of the child will be, is a question of probability. No one is wise enough to forecast, or determine absolutely, what or what would not be best for it; yet we have to act upon these probabilities from the testimony before us, guided by the ordinary laws of human experience. [*Chapsky* v. *Wood*, 26 Kan. Report 650, 654–55 (1881)]

In 1958, a Missouri appellate court also examined the basis for a presumption. The court rejected a mother's claim over a father's for the custody of their two children, ages eight and five. The court said:

Although our courts have said many times that, *"all other things being equal,"* custody of a child of tender years should be awarded to the mother . . ., the paramount and controlling consideration in every child custody case, to which all other principles and presumptions must yield is the welfare of the child. . . . There is no paucity of cases demonstrating that, where the best interests of a child will be served thereby, custody will be awarded to the father; and, clearly this should be and is true even where both parents are fit and proper persons to rear the child. [*Ragan* v. *Ragan*, 315 S.W.2d 142, 147 (1958)]

24. For instance, under the guidelines set forth in *Before the Best Interest of the Child,* court and counsel in deciding whether to remove *older* children from long-term caretakers and return them to their natural parents would need clinical assessments of the child and the interested adults to assure the best available disposition for the child:

> For some children in the older age group, the statutory period of 24 months or more, no matter how strong the wish of the longtime caretakers to keep "their" child, may not be a sufficient basis for terminating the legal relationships to absent parents who wish to regain custody. Some older children may hold emotional attachments to absent parents all the more fiercely and possessively the longer the separation lasts. Their early, long-standing, psychological ties, even though not assisted by current experience, may interfere with the formation of new psychological attachments to the fostering adults no matter how genuine their affection may be or how real the satisfaction they offer.

> *   *   *

> To protect such children and their legal parents from unjustified dispositions, this ground provides a special hearing of any child over 5 years of age,
>
> (a) who, at the time of placement, had been in continuous care of his parents for not less than the 3 preceding years; *and*
> (b) who had *not* been separated from his par-

ents because they inflicted or attempted to inflict serious bodily injury upon him or were convicted of a sexual offense against him.

Drawing upon the best available professional personnel, and recognizing the limits of such inquiries, the hearing would be designed to determine whether the child's absent parents are still his psychological parents and whether his return to them would be the least detrimental alternative. [*Id.* at pp. 47–48]

Under many statutory schemes experts would continue to be engaged because their training has equipped them with the skill to understand and interpret the language of children. They may be able to throw light on the needs and wishes of children and thus, where these are relevant, prepare the judge to make informed placement decisions. See footnote 30 and accompanying text in Chapter 3.

Expert testimony may also be required because:

[A] judge's experience may be very limited and, even if not limited, be capable of expansion by expert evidence which is itself a compendious way of expanding experience, theory being, if sound, the condensation and refinement of the experience of many minds. One can only compare the understanding of the child since the concept of childish innocence has been replaced by an understanding of infant sexuality to which, to my knowledge, the general knowledge and experience of judges did not contribute, to appreciate that judges even in their special fields have to be free to utilize the evidence of the learned. [Hutley, J. J. A. in *Epperson* v. *Dampney* (1976), 10 Australian Law Review 227, 232]

25. *Beyond the Best Interests of the Child* (pp. 175–76).

26. *Ross* v. *Hoffman,* 372 A.2d 582, 594 (Md., 1977).

27. A practical child advocate has suggested that Dr. Hague's report might be better received if it began by suggesting that daytime visits would be preferable to overnight visits, and then went on to explain why it would be better for Jane if there were no order of visitation.

28. Additional tests may pose a specific threat to a child. In Chapter 6 Dr. James explains why he decided against continuing interviews because of the threat they posed to the child.

29. See *Beyond the Best Interests of the Child* (p. 66).
    Confronted with a dilemma similar to that of Dr. Burns, another child psychoanalyst tried to use his report to the court to "educate" the judge who had restricted the scope of inquiry in a way which precluded a professionally complete examination. The psychoanalyst abided by the judge's restrictions but prefaced his report with a paragraph chastising the judge. He wrote: "In all my years of working with the courts this is the first time I have ever seen such an order." The judge did not follow his recommendation.

30. The Report is reproduced in *Before the Best Interests of the Child* (Appendix I, p. 144 *et seq.*).

31. "[This] was *not* a moment which they [the social workers of the child care agency] would have chosen to hand Maria back" (*id.* at p. 159, par. 62; emphasis supplied).

32. *Ibid.* Presumably the social workers believed that they needed to be on good terms with Maria's mother and stepfather to continue serving Maria. See Chapter 5.

33. *Report*, reproduced in *Before the Best Interests of the Child* (Appendix I, p. 159, par. 62).

34. We question the appropriateness of allowing the same judge to preside at both the pretrial hearing where probable outcomes are discussed and the hearing on the case proper.

35. See also text in Chapter 3 following footnote 35.

    We also recognize that limited financial and personnel resources of child care agencies and legal service agencies may make the likelihood of prevailing a factor in efficiently allocating resources. But such resource restraints should not be allowed to obscure the extent to which the interests of the child may be disserved.

    A Connecticut judge emphasized the importance of social workers' pursuing the interests of the child:

    > When I instruct new . . . social workers, I urge them to seek the relief they feel is indicated, and if it is rejected let the buck stop at the judge's bench where the action taken (or denied) is on the record, appealable, and *visible*. . . . [It] is disheartening when time after time [their requests] are denied by judges acting out of ig-

> norance and seat-of-the-pants "expertise," but if the agency does not try for the action that may save the child from further harm, there is *no* chance that such action will be taken. [Letter from Hon. Frederica S. Brenneman to Albert J. Solnit (November 24, 1982)]

36. See Henry M. Hart, Jr. and John T. McNaughton, "Evidence and Inference in Law," 87 *Daedalus* 40, 53–54 (Winter 1958):

> ... The issues of fact arise out of the law but, at the point of application of law, the issues of law also arise out of the facts. This chicken-and-egg relationship exists in any case in which indeterminacy in the law must be resolved; and such cases are innumerable. The difficulty obviously is acute when both law and facts are uncertain and in dispute. The difficulty in this acute form is especially worth calling to the attention of an audience of nonlawyers because it lies at the heart of the trouble which lawyers and specialists in other disciplines continually have when they try to work together, particularly in the preparation and trial of litigated cases.
> ... The court or agency does not have a completely free hand in the resolution of indeterminacies in the applicable law; it must relate its decision in reasoned fashion to principles and policies already settled and to analogous applications of these principles and policies. A trained lawyer will have a sense of what leeway exists. These and other considerations suggest that the lawyer should be in command of strategic planning in preparing ... such a case, [one

involving a dispute about a child placement, for example] and tell the [child development specialist, for example] what is and is not worthwhile to look for.

But this plainly will not do—at least not without material qualification. For the [child psychologist] is the expert in observing . . . behavior and appraising . . . effects, and he must have some degree of freedom in making his observations and appraisal. Again and again he will notice . . . phenomena which the lawyer would miss but which, when called to the lawyer's attention, will seem to alter the character of the legal problem. So the truth is that neither can be in complete command. They have to learn how to work together, each aware of the indispensability of the other, and each having a sense of the other's potential contribution in developing the analysis.

CHAPTER 5: DUAL ROLE—AMBIGUITY AND AMBIVALENCE

1. See, e.g., Lyon and Levine, "Ethics, Power, and Advocacy," 6 *Law and Human Behavior* 65, 74–77 (1982); "Note, Rehabilitation, Investigation and the Welfare Home Visit," 79 *Yale Law Journal* 746, 751 (1970); Stone, "Psychiatric Abuse and Legal Reform," 5 *International Journal of Law and Psychiatry* 9 (1982); Burt, "Constitution of the Family," 1979 *Supreme Court Review,* 329; American Bar Association *Model Code of Professional Responsibility* particularly Canon 7, pp. 36–46 (1979); *Model Rules of Professional Conduct* (adopted by A.B.A. in August 1983); Freedman,

"The Traditional Relationship between Lawyer and Client Should Be Retained in Ethical Rules," 68 *American Bar Association Journal* 429 (1982); Guggenheim, "The Right to Be Represented but Not Heard: Reflections on Legal Representation for Children," 59 *New York University Law Review* 76 (1984).

2. See, e.g., Justice Blackmun's opinion for the court in *Wyman* v. *James,* 400 U.S. 309 (1971), in which he characterizes home visits under a program of Aid to Families with Dependent Children as "both rehabilitative and investigative" (*id.* at 317). Justice Blackmun observes:

> The visit is not one by police or uniformed authority. It is made by a caseworker of some training whose primary objective is, or should be, the welfare, not the prosecution, of the aid recipient for whom the worker has profound responsibility. As has already been stressed, the program concerns dependent children and the needy families of those children. It does not deal with crime or with the actual or suspected perpetrators of crime. The caseworker is not a sleuth but rather, we trust, is a friend to one in need. [*Id.* at 322–23]

For a discussion of this romantic vision of the relationship between the social worker as authority and the welfare applicant as dependent, see Burt, "Forcing Protection on Children and Their Parents: The Impact of Wyman v. James," 69 *Michigan Law Review* 1259 (1971).

For another romantic view—a failure to recognize the dual role implications—see Australian Family

Court Judge Watson's description of the functions of a welfare officer ordered to supervise visits:

> The intention of this order is not that such welfare officer should police my orders in the same manner as a probation officer or a child welfare officer may have done in the past. It is, however, the intention of this order that all parties ... having any relationship with these children, that is the father, the mother, the uncle and the aunt may have available to them a properly trained resource person to whom they can turn and discuss problems and difficulties.
>
> I would point out to the parties that any conferences that take place under sec. 62 of the Act are completely privileged from later disclosure. No report can come back to the court of what happens at such conferences or what is said and such conferences are to be treated as completely confidential.
>
> On the other hand I would further point out that by making an order under sec. 64(5) I have placed in the hands of a welfare officer the ability on his own motion if he considers that the children are not being properly treated by the parties or by others on his own motion to bring the matter back before the court to invite the court to consider other orders. [*Bainrot and Bainrot* (1976), FLC 75,062, 75,064]

3. See Chapter 3, pp. 26–27.

4. See *Before the Best Interests of the Child* (Appendix I, p. 141).

5. For some confirming views and supporting evidence concerning lawyers, see, *e.g.*, editorial in *Wall Street Journal* (August 15, 1983) on A.B.A. proposed, but rejected, code clause defining when lawyers should "report a client's mischievous intent to law enforcement authorities":

> [While] lawyers are technically described as officers of the court, we have seen very few persuasive arguments that this means the same thing as being agents of the state. . . . The practical effect of a whistle-blowing provision would be to induce lawyers to focus their attention and spend their time not on their client's legal problems, but on their own.

See Chief Justice Burger in *Trammel* v. *United States* 445 U.S. 40 (1980) on the "imperative need for confidence and trust" between lawyer and client so as to enable the lawyer to provide effective assistance:

> The lawyer–client privilege rests on the need for the advocate and counselor to know all that related to the client's reasons for seeking representation if the professional mission is to be carried out. [*Id.* at 51]

For a somewhat different view of the implications of the A.B.A. proposal see Burt, "Conflict and Trust between Attorney and Client," 69 *Georgetown Law Journal* 1015 (1981). Concerning doctors see Walker, "Mental Cruelty Check Urged on Children," *London Observer* (July 31, 1980):

> Dr. Tony Keable-Elliott, a member of the GP's National Committee, said: "In my view, the parents should always be informed, but you run

the risk of alienating them. I am a doctor not
only to the child but also to the parents. If I
say to a parent 'I think you have battered your
child' and I am wrong, I will have destroyed the
doctor–patient relationship and that parent
won't come to me again."

Dr. Keable-Elliott claims that the fear of
being reported is so strong that, in one case he
knew, a mother kept her bruised child away
from school in case she was accused of batter-
ing. Despite the official advice, he said, doctors would keep the decision whether to inform
on their patients as a matter of individual conscience.

We do not examine the dual role problem in-
herent in state laws requiring pediatricians, for instance, to report cases of suspected child abuse.
However, these professionals should, at the outset of
their relationship, inform parents of their patients of
the limits to confidentiality imposed by such laws. (See
Before the Best Interests of the Child, pp. 71, 135,
320.)

Concerning social workers, see Faller, "Unan-
ticipated Problems in the United States Child Protection System," 9 *Child Abuse & Neglect,* 63–69 (1985).
Knowing that they will be legally bound to report in-
stances of client wrongdoing, conscientious social
workers inform their clients that anything disclosed in
their meetings could be used against them by those in
authority. Such a warning would do much to undermine the relationship of confidence and trust necessary for effective counseling and would close the
channels of communication. Intentional "ignorance"
could also result. Faller describes how one social
worker, for example, advised her clients, parents, both

of whom were sexually abusing their child, not to give her information about the abuse lest she have to report them *(ibid.)*. And see Graham, "Civil Liberties Problems in Welfare Administration," 43 *New York University Law Review* 836, 853 (1968), which describes the results of an empirical study of welfare administration in two Metropolitan New York counties:

> [It] is considered unusual for caseworkers to attempt physical searches of clients' apartments. [Most] recipients believe that some caseworkers want to avoid reporting evidence of fraud for considerations of personal safety, to avoid extra paper work, or out of sympathy for the client. Frequently . . . a worker will ignore indications that a man is present in a . . . home.

Also see A. J. Solnit, "Too Much Reporting, Too Little Service: Roots and Prevention of Child Abuse," *Child Abuse—An Agenda for Action*, ed. G. Gerbner, C. J. Ross, and E. Zigler (New York and Oxford: Oxford University Press, 1980, pp. 135–146).

6. The therapeutic or working alliance refers to "the relatively nonneurotic, rational rapport which the patient has with the analyst. It is this reasonable and purposeful part of the feelings the patient has for the analyst which makes for the *working alliance*." See Ralph R. Greenson, *The Technique and Practice of Psychoanalysis,* Vol. 1 (New York: International Universities Press, 1967, pp. 192–93). Striving to establish a neutral environment in which he and his patient can work together, the therapist (clinician) comes to be known by his patient not only as a trusting, em-

pathic, and accepting (nonmoralistic) professional but also as a particular individual. Under these conditions the patient is free enough to remember and transfer significant past attitudes and expectations on to the therapist, i.e., to create transferences, which is a crucial aspect of the therapeutic process. Thus, a working or therapeutic alliance is established as a result of the patient's experience with and perception of the therapist as a trusted person who is interested in him. Conversely, the therapeutic alliance is a reflection of the therapist's experiences with the patient as a unique person who is trying to understand and to cope with his difficulties, and who learns to work with the therapist.

The therapeutic alliance also implies that patient and therapist agree to respect the patient's confidentiality and autonomy as essential components of the patient's well-being. A clinician who carries out an evaluation in the context of a child placement conflict cannot establish a therapeutic or working alliance because of the lack of confidentiality and because the aim of the evaluation is to answer questions raised by the court and the parties to the dispute. Also see S. Freud, "The Dynamics of Transference," 12 *S.E.*, 97–108 (1912); Elizabeth Zetzel, "Current Concepts of Transference," 37 *International Journal of Psychoanalysis*, 369–76 (1945); Hans W. Loewald, "On the Therapeutic Action of Psychoanalysis," 41 *International Journal of Psychoanalysis*, 16–33 (1960); Leo Stone, *The Psychoanalytic Situation* (New York: International Universities Press, 1961).

7. *Report of Professor J. D. McClean Concerning Karen Spencer to the Derbyshire County Council and Derbyshire Area Health Authority,* ¶1.1 (1978).

8. *Ibid.*

9. *Id.* at ¶2.124.

10. *Id.* at ¶2.118–119.

11. Reproduced in *id.* at ¶2.120.

12. *Id.* at ¶2.122.

13. *Id.* at ¶2.123. Professor McClean added: " . . . I sense that a little optimism was thought to be essential if the Spencers were to be given a sense of purpose and direction."

14. *In the Matter of: Roy M. C., Jennifer C., Shannon C., and Jason C. and in the Matter of: The Child Welfare Act Part II* [1980] 14 R.F.L. 2d 21 (Provincial Dist. Ct. [Fam. Div.] of the Judicial District of York).

15. *Id.* at 2, 4 (slip opinion) (emphasis supplied). The judge assigned the same potentially conflicting roles to lawyers for adults:

> All counsel have the duty of advocating and expressing the instructions, views and preferences of their clients, be they parents, children or societies, but they also have the professional and social duty of ensuring that all *relevant* evidence is adduced, that no such evidence is suppressed, and further, to be prepared to give an honest and *professional* statement of what they feel is in the best interest of the child and the reasons for that position. . . . I can see no practical difficulties with this role for counsel. [*Id.* at 6; emphasis supplied]

Not unlike the consultant psychiatrist in the Karen Spencer case who mistakenly thought he could take a "global view" and represent the interests of both parent and child in a placement proceeding are the views attributed to Samuel Schoonmaker III, a divorce lawyer who is reported to have spoken of some misunderstandings in the expectations of parents as to the attorney–client relationship. " 'In a state like Connecticut,' he said, 'counsel for the children is very rare, so that divorce lawyers like me feel that we have a double duty to represent that child, who did not hire us, as well as the adult who did. I tell the parent clients this, and I say that there will be restrained advocacy,' Schoonmaker explained. 'This is somewhat contra-dictory, of course. You are to a degree trying to play the judge. Vigorous representation in a custody con-test,' he said, 'is something a lawyer ought not to do, and I put this in writing . . .' " (5 *Family Law Re-porter* 869, Sept. 4, 1979; see also *id.* at 2948).

16. *Re. W.*, 13 F.R.L. (2d) 381 (1979).

17. *Id.* at 382.

18. *Id.* at 384.

Judge Abella said that the lawyer's role of *counselor* to his client is not inconsistent with his role as advocate of the client's wishes. At the same time she warned that in the case of the child client, lawyers must be especially sensitive to the danger of abusing their counseling role:

> In the case of a child who is capable of coherent expression the lawyer's role in representing the child's wishes does not preclude the lawyer from exploring with the child the merits or real-

ities of the case, evaluating the practicalities of the child's position and even offering, where appropriate, suggestions about the possible reasonable resolutions to the case. Offering advice is part of the lawyer's obligation to protect the client's interests. Obviously, however, given the vulnerability of most children to authority in general and given the shattered sensibilities in family disputes in particular, great sensitivity should be exercised during these exploratory sessions. [*Id.* at 385]

19. *Id.* at 383.

20. *Before the Best Interests of the Child* (pp. 112–22). For a different view see P. K. Milmed, "Due Process for Children: A Right to Counsel in Custody Proceedings," 4 *New York University Review of Law & Social Change* 177, 187–88 (Spring 1974):

Regardless of whether the child or the attorney more correctly perceives what is in fact better for the child, the constitutional purpose of providing a person with representation is to enable him effectively to present *his* views to the court. The fourteenth amendment does not require the "best" result for the person whose interests are at stake; rather, it requires that a person be heard in proceedings which affect his interests. Since in custody proceedings the child's interests are at stake, due process requires that *his* preferences be expressed and considered.

See also (particularly with regard to the role of lawyers for older children over 7 years) Guggenheim, "The Right to Be Represented but Not Heard: Reflections on Legal Representation for Children, 59 *New York University Law Review* 76, 117 *et seq.* (1984).

21. *Re. W., supra* n.16, at 385.

22. *Ibid.*

23. See *Before the Best Interests of the Child* (p. 22) and *Beyond the Best Interests of the Child* (p. 66).

24. See Note, "Rehabilitation, Investigation and the Welfare Home Home Visit," 79 *Yale Law Journal* 746, 759 (1970), which argues that because a welfare home visit combines both a personal, rehabilitative function and an investigative one, "the only cure for welfare administration is the complete separation of services and investigation throughout the system."

CHAPTER 6: NO LICENSE TO ACT AS PARENTS

1. Wendell Berry, *The Unsettling of America: Culture & Agriculture* (New York: Avon, 1978 p. 45).

2. The ability to locate the line between the usurper of parental autonomy and the caring expert distinguishes the professional from relatives and neighbors who do not mind their own business.

   Of course, if parents choose to delegate to a day care center the role of raising their child, the professionals there do not exceed their authority by assuming a parental role. The freedom to delegate child care to others is within the license granted to parents on how to raise their children—even if it means substituting the specialist for the generalist. See *Before the*

Best Interests of the Child (pp. 40–45) and *Beyond the Best Interests of the Child* (p. 48) on how short-term child care, once it becomes long-term, may create a parent–child relationship.

3. From his training and experience the professional person knows that his care, guidance, and teaching of children should reflect an awareness that parents are the most important adults in the child's life. See Provence and Naylor, *Working with Disadvantaged Parents and Their Children* (New Haven: Yale University Press, 1983), p. 4:

> We were influenced in our choice of both services and methods of study by the view that those closest to the child, his parents, exert the strongest influence on his development and that his development would be best followed, protected and promoted by the study staff through a continuing and close association with his parents—a partnership in behalf of the child.

Parents or legal guardians may delegate to the expert the responsibility for providing specialized services. In giving his services, the professional therapist invites the child's "transference" of feelings, attitudes, expectations, and behaviors that are displaced from the parents. He is supposed to be aware of his own "transference" to the child—the emergence of feelings and attitudes that grow out of his own past and that are triggered by the child who is his client, or by the child's parents. Acknowledged and understood, these residues of significant past relationships can be used by the professional in the service of the child. Ignoring them, however, the professional risks acting on them to serve his own unresolved, unconscious needs at the child's expense. See Anna Freud, "Normality and Pathology in Childhood," in *The Writings of Anna Freud,* Vol. VI (New York: International Universities Press, 1965); Anna Freud, Joseph Sandler, and Robert L. Tyson, *et al., The Technique of Child Psychoanalysis* (Cambridge, Mass: Harvard University Press, 1980); Sigmund Freud, "Constructions in Analysis," 23 *S. E.,* 255-69 (1937).

4. See, e.g., *Beck* v. *Beck*, 86 N.J. 480, 432 A.2d 63, 71 (1981).

5. Professionals teaching, treating, or taking care of children at the request of parents frequently become important adults to such children, especially the younger, more dependent ones. For example, a child in nursery school who has the same teacher for a year or more may become strongly attached to him. Such attachments are secondary in strength to the primary relationship children normally have with "ordinary devoted parents." These secondary relationships continue into kindergarten and the first, second, and third grades, often with one teacher who is felt to be special. For the five- or six-year-old child, that teacher is the one who also may evoke the feelings and hopes that were directed toward the parents a year or two earlier. Such displacements are most clearly detectable when the child is seeing a therapist several times a week. Certain of these important adults become the persons to whom the child transfers part of his deeply felt wishes, affection, hopes, fears, and other attitudes and behaviors that originated within and are still part of the ongoing primary child–parent relationship. Such transferences are a vital aspect of psychoanalytic treatment, where they can be verbalized and played out, made explicit, clarified and worked through:

I now agree fully that during analytic treatment children regard their analyst not only as a new object for their affectionate or hostile, sexual or aggressive impulses, or as a helping person with whom they can establish a working alliance, but that, with therapy conducted within the correct limits, multitudes of transference phenomena appear, either additional to or instead of the same impulses and behavioral attitudes that the child displayed toward his original objects. [*The Writings of Anna Freud*, Vol. I (New York: International Universities Press, 1974, p. xii)]

6. See Jill Tweedie, "Society Does Not Care What Happens to the Clients of Social Workers," *The Guardian* (London) March 29, 1979, at 3:

... I vividly remember a programme I once saw about a social worker and the children she tended in a home. She talked most touchingly of the special relationship she had established with a particularly difficult child and how much it meant to him. She then mentioned that she was about to leave this job and this child because she wanted to take a further course in child psychology.

I presume the course would have emphasized the vital importance for any child of a long-term adult relationship and this nice social worker would have taken notes and passed her examination *summa cum laude*. But the child would have been better off if she had been less ambitious, less bright, less able to take such a course and, therefore, remained with him until he had grown up.

See also Anna Freud, "Termination of Treatment," in
Joseph Sandler, Hansi Kennedy, and Robert L. Tyson, *The Technique of Child Psychoanalysis: Discussions with Anna Freud* (Harvard University Press,
1980, p.246); and John Bowlby, *The Making and
Breaking of Affectional Bonds* (London: Tavistock
Publications, 1979). Experiences of children being separated from a person who fulfills the parental role and
whom they love, "especially if repeated, lead to a sense
of being unloved, deserted, and rejected" (*id.,* at p. 10).
Bowlby continues:

> It is these sentiments which are expressed in
> the tragicomic poems of an eleven-year-old de-
> linquent boy whose mother had died when he
> was fifteen months old, and who had thence-
> forward experienced several substitute moth-
> ers . . . :
>
> > *Jumbo had a baby dressed in green,*
> > *Wrapped it up in paper and sent it to the
> > Queen.*
> > *The Queen did not like it because it was
> > too fat,*
> > *She cut it up in pieces and gave it to the
> > cat.*
> > *The cat did not like it because it was too
> > thin,*
> > *She cut it up in pieces and gave it to the
> > King.*
> > *The King did not like it because it was
> > too slow,*
> > *Threw it out the window and gave it to
> > the crow.*
>
> Later, when his therapist was going on holiday,
> he expressed his despair of ever being loved in

the words of the traditional ditty:

> *Oh, my little darling, I love you;*
> *Oh, my little darling, I don't believe you*
> *do.*
> *If you really loved me, as you say you*
> *do,*
> *You would not go to America and leave*
> *me at the zoo.* [*Id.* at pp. 10–11]

On the need for trustworthy relationships with older children in a community living center see Elizabeth Sturz, *Widening Circles* (New York: Harper & Row, 1983, p. 149):

> Being in the "people business" is a little like being a priest or doctor. If you can't adhere to the ethics of the profession, you had better find another way to earn a living. Many of our youngsters feel that the significant adults in their lives have let them down. We should not add to that disappointment and betrayal. How we conduct ourselves is crucial in getting through to the young people we work with; living up to our own rules is a part of our method.

7. Justice Murray in *Emotional Needs of Infants and Young Children: Implications for Policy and Practice,* ed. Graham Martin (Adelaide, South Australia: AWCH, 1979, p. 251). On lawyers not acting as parents see *Before the Best Interests of the Child* (pp. 112–15, 123–26).

8. *In the Matter of Melissa M.,* 421 N.Y.S.2d 300, 101 Misc. 2d 407 (1979).

9. *Id.* at 304. The court had earlier rejected the psychiatrists' recommendation that Melissa should remain with her foster parents (*id.* at 301). We would have supported that recommendation, see *Before the Best Interests of the Child* (pp. 39–57).

10. These problems are examined in *Beyond the Best Interests of the Child* (pp. 116–33) and *Before the Best Interests of the Child* (pp. 31–129). See also excerpt from *Autobiography of Malcolm X,* Appendix II.

11. An analogous situation arises when a judge promises confidentiality and either does not keep his promise or keeps the promise and thereby prevents proper conduct of the case. See *H* v. *H,* 1 All E. R. 1145, 1147 (1974) (Megaw, L. J.):

> In an unreported case, *B* v. *S,* the judge, who had interviewed the children concerned, had made clear on the outside of the envelope which was submitted to this court, and in the notes of the hearing which were submitted to this court, the unequivocal promise [of confidentiality] that he had given to the children. In my judgment the situation here is the same, the only difference being that here, because of the absence of a warning of the nature of the promise that had been given, the envelope had been opened and seen by one member of the court before the position was realised. It is most unfortunate for the parties. It is most unfortunate for the children.
> It is of course often most desirable in [custody disputes] that the judge hearing the case should see the children and should see the children otherwise than in open court. One can

well understand that in matters of this sort the
children may be reluctant to express themselves freely and frankly when there is the possibility that what they say may be made known,
and perhaps particularly made known to their
parents. It is of course desirable in the highest
degree that when children are seen in this way,
not in open court, every possible step should be
taken to ensure that what they say should be
said freely and frankly. Nevertheless in my
judgment it is wrong that a judge should give
a promise to a child such as was given in . . .
the present case. Of course the concern of the
court in these matters is the welfare of the children. It is certainly possible that when a judge
sees the children in private, something may
emerge which requires to be further investi-
gated as a matter of necessity for the benefit
of the children themselves; and that may in-
volve the necessity of a judge disclosing that
which he has heard. How can he do that if he
has made a promise to the children at the outset that nothing they say will be disclosed to
anyone? Further, there is the position of this
court. There is an appeal as of right from the
judge's decision. This court has to arrive at a
conclusion affecting the welfare of the children
and decide whether the judge was right or
wrong. How can this court discharge the task
if something which may have been important
in the judge's decision is something of which
this court cannot make itself aware without
breaking a solemn promise given by a judge to
the person who supplied the information?

    It seems to me that in this extraordinarily difficult situation, while the judge seeing the child privately must naturally do all he can to encourage the child to speak freely, frankly and without fear, he may not give the child a promise which would be such in its terms, or be understood by the child as meaning, that in no circumstances will anything that the child says be made known to anyone else.

12. In a custody visitation case, a trial judge's order that "all future proceedings . . . be brought before him personally and not before any other judge" was held to be beyond his power. In *Re Marriage of Mathews*, 101 Cal.App. 3d 816, 161 Cal. Rptr. 879, 881 (1980) citing as controlling the California Supreme Court in *People* v. *Osslo*, 50 Cal.2d 75, 104, 323 P.2d 397, 413 (1958):

> An individual judge (as distinguished from a court) is not empowered to retain jurisdiction of a cause. The cause is before the court, not the individual judge of that court, and the jurisdiction which the judge exercises is the jurisdiction of the court, not of the judge. Rules of court which provide that posttrial proceedings in a cause shall be heard by the judge who tried the matter are entirely proper, but the individual judge cannot order that such proceedings must be heard by him.

13. See *Before the Best Interests of the Child* (pp. 123–26).

14. *Ibid.* On parents as insulation for a child "from direct contact with the law" see *id.* at 32, 113–14, and 259. On lawyer and therapist recognizing that they are not

licensed to be parents see Charlie's case, *id.* at 118–21. On a judge in effect licensing a lawyer to act as parent see discussion of *G.* v. *G., id.* at 123–26.

15. When a child has grown attached to "short-term" foster parents, separation from them is bound to cause him distress—a distress that will be repeated when the child has had multiple placements. The experience of the Hampstead Nurseries which provided care for children whose parents could not look after them for a variety of war-related reasons provides examples of the confusion and turmoil experienced by children under such circumstances:

> Reggie had come to the Hampstead Nurseries as a baby of five months, went home to his mother when he was twenty months, and returned to the Nursery two months later. While he was at the Nursery:

>> [He] formed two passionate relationships to two young nurses who took care of him at different periods. The second attachment was suddenly broken at 2 years, 8 months when his "own" nurse married. He was completely lost and desperate after her departure, and refused to look at her when she visited him a fortnight later. He turned his head to the other side when she spoke to him, but stared at the door, which had closed behind her, after she had left the room. In the evening in bed he sat up and said: "My very own Mary Ann. But I don't like her!" [Anna Freud, "Infants Without Families: Reports on the Hampstead Nurseries 1939–1945," in *The Writings of Anna Freud,* Vol. III (New York: International Universities Press, 1973, p. 596)]

But the fact that such separations are bound to happen is not an argument against foster parents caring for children with warmth and love.

> When choosing between the two evils of broken and interrupted attachments and an existence of emotional barrenness, the latter is the more harmful solution because . . . it offers less prospect for normal character development. [*Ibid.*]

16. See J. Goldstein, "Why Foster Care—For Whom for How Long?" in 30 *The Psychoanalytic Study of the Child,* 647, 658–660 (1975); and *Before the Best Interests of the Child* (pp. 39–51).

17. Outside of the child placement process, judges and lawyers more easily recognize when other professionals infringe upon parental choice. When, for example, a county jail banned visits from the children of inmates because "the jailer [believed] that it is not in the best interests of the children to visit their parents . . . in jail," the court declared the ban unrelated to any legitimate function of the jail (*Valentine* v. *Englehardt,* 474 F. Supp. 294, 301 [1979]). The court said that deciding the best interests of the inmates' children "simply does not lie with jail officials" (*id.* at 302). But see excerpt from *Autobiography of Malcolm X,* Appendix II.

18. See Chapter 5.

19. It is not unusual for a psychiatric report to a court to contain a closing statement like:

> I strongly recommend further treatment *on a voluntary basis* for Richard, and for Richard

and Mrs. Cross (his grandmother who has been taking care of him), and for Richard and his parents. Any insight obtained could improve the quality of their lives and subsequently Richard's.

The "on a voluntary basis" does not negate the intrusiveness of such statements. To suggest that the court join in giving such advice—which it sometimes does in a placement order—is likely to deprive *voluntary* of any real meaning.

20. See *Before the Best Interests of the Child* (pp. 58–109).

21. Remarks of Richard Chilsom, in *The Emotional Needs of Infants and Young Children, supra* n.7, p. 252.

22. See *Beyond the Best Interests of the Child* (pp. 113–33) and *Before the Best Interests of the Child* (pp. 91–109).

23. On the principles of *least intrusive invocation, least intrusive adjudication,* and *least intrusive disposition,* see *Before the Best Interests of the Child* (pp. 24–25, and n.*, at p. 90).

CHAPTER 7: SOFTHEARTED AND HARDHEADED

1. Chapter 6, p. 95 and Chapter 1, p. 5.

2. See, e.g., Chapter 5, n.13 and accompanying text.

3. Chapter 6, p. 99.

4. Wendell Berry, *The Unsettling of America: Culture and Agriculture* 31 (New York: Avon, 1978); Sigmund Freud, "On Beginning the Treatment" (*S. E.*, 12:121–44 [1958]); and see Chapter 6, n.7 and accompanying text. Other illustrations of the dehumanization of "humanness"—of the robotization of "personal interest"—are provided by the judge who after sentencing a person to a term of years in prison is alleged to have said, "Have a good day," and by the person at the supermarket check-out counter who greets each customer with a big smile under a sign proclaiming "No charge if the cashier doesn't give you a smile."

5. See, e.g., Stone, Tyler, and Mead, "Law Enforcement Officers as Investigators and Therapists in Child Sexual Abuse: A Training Model," 8 *Child Abuse & Neglect*, 75 (1984):

> The police officer is frequently the first person to respond to a report of child sexual abuse and, therefore, bears a heavy responsibility. Sensitive treatment and understanding of the child by the first officer on the scene will affect the victim positively and may decrease the chances of long-term psychological damage. [*Id.* at 76]

> Despite the suggestion of dual roles for the police in title and text of this article, the training program described seems primarily devoted to the need for the police to incorporate what we call humanness or softheartedness in fulfilling their investigative role when dealing with child victims of sexual abuse and their families.

> A training model for law enforcement personnel should take into consideration . . . (3) the

importance of objective and sensitive interviewing techniques. A thoroughly trained police officer can lessen the traumatization of the
child and family.

The victim's physical and mental well-
being must always be the police officer's first
responsibility and concern. An officer who
overreacts to the assault or acts in a punitive
manner towards the offender could retrauma-
tize the victim and add to the long-term psychological effects of the abuse.

One major problem experienced by most
persons coming in contact with child sexual
abuse is that they have their own intense feelings about the perpetrators and what they have
done to the child. If these feelings become too
strong, they may interfere with the officer's objective investigation and handling of cases.
This, in turn, may lead to dismissal of the case
because the evidence taken is incomplete or obtained illegally, or the victim was coerced into
distorting facts. A proper understanding and
management of the police officer's reactions
and appropriate training may make the difference between removing the perpetrator from
the situation or releasing him to continue the
sexual misuse of the child. [*Ibid.*]

The child victim is an important individual in the investigation . . . of sexual abuse. The
interview of the child is a critical stage in the
investigation and the results of the police action are in large measure the results of the interview. [*Id.* at 78]

6. Reported in J. Goldstein, "Why Foster Care—For Whom for How Long?" in 30 *The Psychoanalytic Study of the Child,* 647, 656 (1975).

7. Lewis, I. C., "Humanizing Paediatric Care," 7 *Child Abuse & Neglect,* 413, 414 (1983).

8. *Ibid.*

9. *Id.* at 417.

10. *Id.* at 415. See also James Robertson on hardhearted hospital policies:

> [As] societies become highly developed there is a constant tendency to push parents aside so that there may be no hinderance to the exercise of specialised skills—ignoring the fact that, whatever skills are available, there is a need to include parents within the system so that the family is sustained as a functioning entity.
>
> The clearest example of the tendency for parents to be undervalued by systems geared to efficiency is to be found in the history of hospital care for young children. In every highly developed society, the battle for hygiene and asepsis was paralleled by the exclusion of parents from the care of their children when sick in hospital.
>
> Fifty years ago it may have seemed reasonable to exclude parents as possible sources of infection; but there was also a linked tendency to denigrate the parents of young pa-

tients as 'nuisances', to criticise them for being 'over-anxious', to wish them away, to believe that child patients were happier and more contented when parents did not visit. [*The Emotional Needs of Infants and Young Children: Implications for Policy and Practice*, Graham Martin, ed. (Adelaide, South Australia: The Association for the Welfare of Children in Hospital, 1979, p. 15)]

11. Anna Freud, "Infants Without Families: Reports on the Hampstead Nurseries, 1939–1945," in *The Writings of Anna Freud*, Vol. III (New York: International Universities Press, 1973, p. 305).

Index

A

Abandonment (case example), 102
Abella, Judge, 89, 203
Abuse, 217–18
  case examples, 35–37, 72–74, 87
Access: *see* Visitation
Addington v. *Texas,* 154, 169, 173
Adjudication vs. legislative facts, 184–87
Administrative Procedure Act, 160–61
Adoption of B. by E. & R., In re, 178
Adoption cases
  by foster parents, 102–103
  professional boundaries recognized in, 39–44
Aki and Edgar (case example), 103–104
Arons, A. B., 184

B

B. v. *S.,* 211
Bainrot and Bainrot, 197
Beck v. *Beck,* 207
Before the Best Interests of the Child, 6, 10–11, 147, 149, 170, 174, 197, 204, 205, 211, 213, 216
  on child placement standards, 155
  Colwell report, 192–93
  on confidentiality in abuse cases, 199
  on disposition guidelines, 181, 183, 190
  on foster care, 215
  on lawyer's role in representing children, 169
  on least detrimental alternative, 5
  on least intrusive principles, 216
  on longtime caretakers, 171